Short Bike Rides™
in Michigan

Short Bike Rides™ Series

Short Bike Rides™ in Michigan

Second Edition

by
Pamela Stovall

The Globe Pequot Press

Old Saybrook, Connecticut

Cover photo: Chris Dubé
All other photos by Pamela Stovall
Cover design: Saralyn D'Amato-Twomey

Short Bike Rides is a trademark of The Globe Pequot Press.

Library of Congress Cataloging-in-Publication Data

Stovall, Pamela.
  Short bike rides in Michigan / by Pamela Stovall.—2nd ed.
      p.   cm. — (Short bike rides series)
  ISBN 0-7627-0210-9
    1. Bicycle touring—Michigan—Guidebooks. 2. Michigan—
  Guidebooks. I. Title. II. Series.
  GV1045.5.M5S86 1998
  796.6'4'09774—dc21
                                                                98-14399
                                                                    CIP

♺ This book is printed on recycled paper.
Manufactured in the United States of America
Second Edition/First Printing

To the most "bazaar" Dennis Stovall

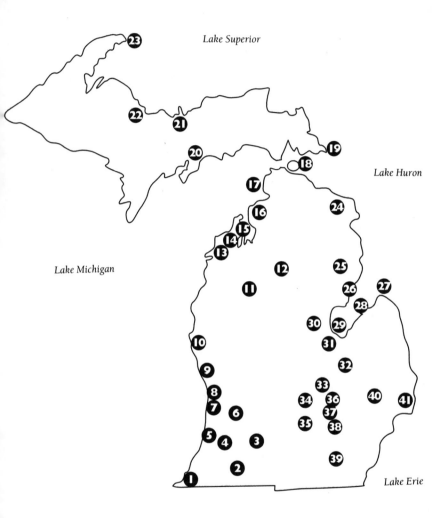

Lake Superior

Lake Huron

Lake Michigan

Lake Erie

Contents

Preface to the Second Edition

Biking in Michigan just keeps getting better—even in the few short years since the first edition of this book was published. Not even urban sprawl can diminish the hundreds and hundreds of miles of great roads and trails for biking. As more and more people ride, they are demanding better roads and paths for biking. And through the good work of several local governments, the League of Michigan Bicyclists, and the Michigan Rails-to-Trails Conservancy, improvements are being made.

The second edition of *Short Bike Rides in Michigan* offers more miles of bike routes than before. And, there are more options to choose from—such as shorter loops—to coincide with your time and ability. All the rides have been updated to reflect road changes and road conditions, and some routes have changed to include better, safer, or more scenic roads. I hope you enjoy these rides as much as I do.

Acknowledgments

This book would not have been possible without the help of many, many people throughout the great State of Michigan, from the generous bike clubs to the kind gentleman who gave me a ride when my car broke down on the way to Paint Creek Trail.

I would like to thank specific people and groups who offered suggestions for rides (although the ultimate blame or credit falls to me).

The Three Oaks Bicycle Museum Tour: The Three Oaks Spokes Bicycle Club, Inc., and all its great work with the Backroads Bikeway bicycle tours and the Bicycle Museum.

The Magical Mystery Tour: The River Country Tourism Council of St. Joseph County and its great work mapping routes in the area.

It's a Grrrreat Ride!: The City of Battle Creek Parks & Recreation Department and its work along with the Michigan Department of Natural Resources and the WK Kellogg Foundation on the Battle Creek Linear Park.

A,B,C,D,E,F,G,H, I Got a Ride in Kalamazoo: Donald Stahlbaum of Paw Paw, who suggested the loop including the Kal-Haven Trail State Park.

South Haven Side Ride: Beth at the Department of Natural Resources in South Haven, who suggested the loop including the Kal-Haven Trail State Park.

Gunning Down at Yankee Springs: David Carr, from Hastings, of the Thornapple Valley Bicycle Club.

The Saugatuck Sashay: An adaptation of a route included in the brochure *Greater Ottawa County Bicycle Route Maps*.

Tulip City Tour: An adaptation of a route included in the leaflet *Park Township Bikepaths*.

The Coast Guard City Tour: An adaptation of a route included in the brochure *Greater Ottawa County Bicycle Route Maps*.

Whitehall-Montague's Old Channel Trail: The staff at the White Lake Area Chamber of Commerce.

Lapping Lake Cadillac: The Cadillac Area Visitor's Bureau.

Three Cs and a Circle: Dick Fultz, of The Bicycle Shop, 200 East Michigan Avenue, Grayling, MI 49738, (517) 348–6868; and the wonderful staff at North Higgins Lake State Park and Civilian Conservation Corps Museum.

The Big Spring: Kitch-iti-Kipi: Bob Elcoate and his son, Chris Elcoate, of The Bicycle Shop in Manistique, 315 Deer Street, Manistique, MI 49854, (800) 554–3434, for the route idea and also a great deal on a new odometer.

The Marquette Amble: From the Prison to Presque Isle: Mike Pryor of Marquette.

A Grand Ride at Presque Isle: Deb Pardike at the Alpena Area Convention and Visitors Bureau.

The Tip o' Thumb Tour; and Inside the Thumb: Caseville and the Lake Huron Loop: Tom of the Thumbs Up Bicycle Club.

R&R in Bay City: The Riverwalk and Rail-Trail Tour: Dawn of the Bay Area Community Foundation.

Riding the Pere Marquette: Jim Mertens, a true friend of the Pere Marquette Rail-Trail; and the Midland County Convention and Visitors Bureau.

Saginaw Sashay: Jack Smith, City of Saginaw Parks/Facility Management.

The Clio Creek Circuit: George Atkins, of the City of Clio.

The James S. Miner Riverwalk: Carol Vaughn, Owosso Corunna Area Chamber of Commerce, for suggesting the return loop for the riverwalk ride.

A Capital Ride on the Lansing River Trail: Bob Wilson for his ideas on a loop, and the Capital City River Runners for its great work on the river trail.

Jackson's Portage Lake Loop: "Red" Reiter for his maps, ideas, and great enthusiasm.

LakeLands Trail Loop: Village Cyclery, 109 East Main, Pinckney, offered great ideas for the return loop.

To Hell and Back; and One Half of A2: With a Short Cruise Down Easy Street: Anne Becker, of the City of Ann Arbor Bicycle Program, for her maps, suggestions, time, and support.

The Cemetery Tour: Mike Richardson, of the Adrian Maple Wheelers, for great maps and conversation.

The Paint Creek Trail: Linda Gorecki, coordinator for the trail, for enthusiasm and loop ideas; King's Bikes 'n' Things for return loop.

The Algonac Amble: The staff of the Greater Algonac Chamber of Commerce.

Thanks to Cynthia Krupp with the Michigan Department of Transportation System Planning—Bicycling, in Lansing, for ideas and suggestions.

To Elizabeth Taylor at the Globe Pequot Press, who helped deliver the second edition. And last but never least, my friend and favorite editor, Laura Strom.

People who offered a place to park my bicycle: Michael Conlin, Paul Kish, and Rob and Cathy Preston.

Thanks for the support of Mancha's babysitters, Dorie and Howard Stovall; Rick Leonardo; Kim and Donna Jean Preston; Debbie, Phil, Sarah, and Emily Sweeney; Howard, Audrey, and Allie Stovall; Naomi Sparks and Al Kaiser; Michele and Craig Baranowski; Bea and Jack Russell; Anna Maria Clark; Robert Lee Braendle; Lorenzo Herman; Al and Sue Geldhof; Jim and Lorraine Christians; Ruth Christians; Susan Johnson; Steve Christians; Jennifer M. Johnson; Joe and Peggy Leonardo; Shirley VanderVeen; Marilyn Reintges; Doris Gillis; Velma and Harley Holben; Sue Howell; Kay and Patty Mitchell; Arnie Smith Alexander; Bonnie Rabideau; Daneen Rabideau; Cindy Manning; Rick Miedema; Rose Idziak; Gail Crider; Bea and Jerry Zuppa; Jeanette Minch; Mary and Tom Bearss; Steve Playter; Ed Sickinger; and Julia and the late Adrian Geldhof.

Introduction

Give glaciers the credit. They're responsible for making Michigan the perfect state for bicycling: gently rolling hills; sweeping vistas of four of the Great Lakes; quiet, dense hardwood forests; shimmering lakes, streams, and rivers; and the choice of two peninsulas.

Michigan offers bicyclists coastlines that run longer than the U.S. Eastern Seaboard. There are more than 3,200 miles of the finest white-sand beaches and two scenic national lakeshores. In addition to beautiful beaches to ride along, Michigan's Great Lakes provide cyclists with even more: During the summer the lakes absorb heat, which then slowly dissipates, tempering the state's climate. This moderating effect makes Michigan not only a major fruit-producing state but also a three-season bikers' paradise. Excellent riding can be had from May to October and, for the hardy, from March to November.

American Indians aptly named the state. In the language of the Ojibway, *michi* means "great," and *gan* means "waters." Lake Superior's size makes it the second-largest lake in the world, outsized only by the Caspian Sea. Lakes Huron and Michigan cover enough land to make them the fifth- and sixth-largest lakes in the world.

If the Great Lakes aren't enough water for you, Michigan also has 11,000 smaller lakes and 36,000 miles of rivers and streams. Nowhere in the state are bikers more than 6 miles away from the beauty of water.

If you seek other beautiful scenery, Michigan has that as well. It boasts eighteen million acres of forest, four national forests, twenty-nine state forests, three national parks, and ninety-nine state parks. These are filled with virgin forest, wildlife, sand dunes, and waterfalls. Most are accessible to cyclists and are included in this book.

Away from the crowded thoroughfares, the state has a system of approximately 88,600 miles of county roads. These offer great scenic biking as well as provide access to the recreational areas in the state.

Would you expect anything less from the state that was the first to establish roadside picnic tables?

About the Rides

Unearthing the best forty-one short bicycle rides in Michigan was like trying to find a leaf in a forest—choosing only forty-one was the hardest part. To narrow the field, I talked with members of bicycle clubs throughout the state, looked for routes that included some unique features, and relied on my twenty-two years of personal experience traveling in my home state.

The rides range from 7 to approximately 30 miles and range from easy to challenging, although almost all rides are manageable for the occasional rider. You can enjoy these rides whether your tires are thin or fat; however, the routes are selected with touring bikes in mind. As such, the rides include paved roads, paths, and trails or other surfaces so well maintained that you can take them at a fairly fast clip on a touring bike.

For interest and ease, all forty-one rides are designed as loops, so you see new sites and scenery for the whole ride but don't end up miles from your car. Some rides also offer shorter or longer optional loops to accommodate your interest, energy, or available time.

Each ride includes a map; information on length, pedaling time, terrain, where to find food, things to see, and a general description of the ride; directions to the starting point; and detailed mile-by-mile directions. Pedaling times will vary according to your pace and number of stops. Note that in the mile-by-mile directions, county roads are designated by either CR or CO, depending on each county's usage. The rides are numbered beginning in the southwest of Michigan, heading north up the west coast to the Upper Peninsula, and then down the east coast of the state.

Many rides begin at Michigan state parks, as these offer good parking facilities, are located at or near one of the state's wonderful scenic spots, and usually have drinking water and rest rooms. And because of their idyllic locations, the parks are super places to spend time either before or after your ride.

Passes are required for entrance to state parks and recreational areas. An annual pass allows unlimited use for one vehicle to any of these areas all year long; you can also buy a daily pass. Consider buying an annual sticker for your car—the fee is nominal, and nothing feels better than bypassing the long lines and zipping into any state area you choose. Passes are available at the parks, in the sporting goods department of any Meijer store, or you can write to the Department of Natural Resources, Parks and Recreation, P. O. Box 30257, Lansing, MI 48909; or call (517) 373–1270.

Enjoying the Rides

Using the Maps
Be aware that the maps are not drawn to scale; some areas are enlarged in order to show more details. Arrows indicate the direction that the ride follows, according to the ride's description. U.S. highways are indicated by ⬭, state routes by ◯, and county and other routes by ▭. The shorter options for rides are indicated by a broken line. Space constraints made it impossible to include every small street and railroad crossing on the maps, so follow the "Directions at a glance" carefully.

Gearing up
Cycling can certainly be enjoyed without all the latest gadgets and gizmos. For pleasure without the headaches, however, consider investing in a few basics.

Repairs. Repair kits are available at bike stores, or you can buy the items separately at hardware stores. To make almost all but the most serious repairs, carry a spare tube, patch kit, tire irons, a small pump that can be attached to the frame, a crescent wrench, flat- and Phillips-head screwdrivers, a rag, and multipurpose electrical tape.

Water. Water bottles can be attached to the frame and are a necessity for hot, muggy Michigan days.

Locks. Carry a strong lock on rides where you plan to stop. Some people use a chain and padlock, carrying them wrapped around the seat post. Others wouldn't trust their bikes to anything but a U lock and always carry one in a pack. Always remember that it just takes a second to steal a bike. I once saw a man pull a bike out of the back of a truck and ride away on it—with a crowd watching. With quick-release hubs, it's important to secure both wheels and frame to a rack or some other immovable object.

Bags. Gone are the days when you had to stop and wrestle the wind for control of your map. Handlebar bags with transparent pockets on top for maps let you glance down briefly at intersections to let you know which way to turn. You can make photocopies of the maps in this book and slide them into the plastic flap for easy reference. The rest of the book will fit nicely in the bag and will be there to refer to. You may want to purchase a bag large enough for a jacket, food, or a camera. Another good location for carrying a small bag is under the seat; I've found this to be a good place for the tools and spare tube. Except for short trips, try to avoid wearing a backpack because it raises your center of gravity and can unbalance both you and your bike.

Dog repellent. Some people wouldn't ride without it, but I wouldn't ride with it. Others prefer to use the bike pump to swing and scare pooches off, but it's possible to put yourself in more danger by trying to reach down and take the pump off your bike while keeping an eye on the attacking dog. You might, for example, swerve into traffic or off the road and onto a rough gravel shoulder. One option is to outrun the dog (most dogs stop chasing when you leave their territory). Another is to stop and put the bike between you and the dog and walk your bike away. I've had good luck with pedaling fast and shouting a loud "No!" as the dog approaches. Take the approach you're most comfortable with, but be prepared for it in advance. I think that deciding how you'll react when something happens is half the battle.

Glasses. I'm sure that the driver of the car in Jackson didn't intentionally spin his tires and throw gravel in my face, but listening to the "ping, ping" of small stones bouncing off my glasses certainly reminded me of the importance of eye protection. Glasses will also protect you from bugs and can improve your vision on sunny days. And you can attach a rear-view mirror to them, too.

Comfort. You probably don't need to consider comfort on those short rides to the grocery store, but on longer rides it's a must. I used to scoff at those funny-looking bicyclists decked out with all their paraphernalia—I laughed all the way home with my blisters and numb hands. Good bicycle shorts or pants ensure that no chafing seams come between you and the seat and that the material won't bunch up on your legs. You can completely eliminate numb hands with the padding that good gloves provide, combined with foam padding on your handlebars.

Climate. Michigan fits the old saying, "If you don't like the weather, wait a few minutes and it will change." Clouds may disappear and turn a cool day into a scorcher. Those same clouds may suddenly combine for a thunderstorm. Dressing in layers can help, as can carrying a windbreaker. Of course, in Michigan even hazy or cloudy days can offer a painful sunburn, so pack sunscreen. The climate's also great for bugs. If you plan to stop or picnic along the way, applying insect repellent can save the day.

Riding Safely

The checkup. Get familiar with your bike, and check it each time you go out to ride. Make sure that all the nuts and bolts are tight and that the cables are without frays. I almost did a flip over the front of my bike when the handlebars suddenly gave way under me. Sure enough, I had been in a hurry to hit the road and hadn't checked out the bike first. Reading a good book on bike repair will add confidence to your trips; flat tires and thrown chains don't have to mar your rides.

The road. Although I have tried to alert you to any hazards that you might encounter on these rides, gravel piles move, and potholes come and go. Always watch the road ahead of you—sand, oil, and railroad tracks are just some of the things that can cause spills.

Be aware. Always be conscious of your surroundings, especially if you travel alone. For more than twenty-two years I have traveled all over the state by myself and never had any problems; however, I keep an eye on the conditions in which I find myself. Watch for problem areas or situations, and consider riding with a friend or a group.

Summer travel. If you plan to travel a long distance for a ride, call ahead and check on road conditions and construction in the area to avoid disappointment.

Intersections. One of the most dangerous parts of any ride is an intersection, whether you have the right-of-way or not. Use caution for cars turning right on red lights or turning right in front of you. Left turns by bicyclists are also hazardous. Always be alert and cautious here.

Parked cars. Many motorists open their doors without checking traffic. Watch out for car doors opening, as well as for drivers pulling into traffic from a parking spot without looking for bicycles first.

Laws. Many bike accidents are caused when the rider fails to obey traffic laws—ignoring stop signs, riding two or more abreast, riding the wrong way on a one-way street, and so on. Observing the laws of the road will help ensure your safety.

Visibility. The first step in preventing accidents is being seen. Always wear bright clothing, regardless of the time of day. At night, wear white or reflective clothing and use a white light in front and a red reflector on the back of the bike. Keep in mind the time of day that you're riding. If you are squinting into the sun, automobile drivers are, too, and it's going to be hard to see a bike. Dusk is another time when it's hard to see clearly. Use the strategy of motorcyclists: Turn your lights on early.

Helmets. Ahhh, the feeling of the wind blowing through your hair. It feels great, but many times the price is high. Please consider wearing a Snell- or ANSI-approved helmet all the time, even on short trips. A helmet goes far to prevent or reduce head injuries.

More Bicycle Information and Organizations

The League of Michigan Bicyclists works hard to promote and advance bicycling statewide. It offers information on bike rides, events, and tours. It also publishes the quarterly magazine *The Michigan Bicyclist*. Write The League of Michigan Bicyclists at P. O. Box 16201, Lansing, MI 48901. For general or membership information, call (517) 394–2453 or (888) MI–BIKES.

The league also produces a brochure annually entitled *Bicycle Touring Michigan*, which is available through the league, the Department of Transportation, and local bike stores. The brochure offers a calendar of bicycle rides and events in Michigan, along with names and numbers of area bicycle clubs.

For copies of the brochures *Michigan Biking Information* and *Biking in Michigan,* write or call the Michigan Department of Transportation, System Planning—Bicycling, Terry Eldred or Cynthia Krupp, P. O. Box 30050, Lansing, MI 48909, (517) 373–9192; or the Michigan Travel Bureau at (800) 5432–YES.

Michigan has a wonderfully active chapter of the Rails-to-Trails Conservancy, a nonprofit organization that transforms abandoned railroad corridors into areas for conservation and recreation. To join or to find out more information on its latest work, write or call the Rails-to-Trails Conservancy of Michigan, 913 West Holmes, Suite 145, Lansing, MI 48910, (517) 393–6022.

Feedback

If you'd like to make a suggestion for a different ride or comment on the ones included in this book, I'd appreciate your ideas. Write me at The Globe Pequot Press, P. O. Box 833, Old Saybrook, CT 06475. Happy trails!

Help Us Keep This Guide Up to Date

Every effort has been made by the author and editors to make this guide as accurate and useful as possible. However, many things can change after a guide is published—establishments close, phone numbers change, facilities come under new management, etc.

We would love to hear from you concerning your experiences with this guide and how you feel it could be made better and be kept up to date. While we may not be able to respond to all comments and suggestions, we'll take them to heart, and we'll also make certain to share them with the author. Please send your comments and suggestions to the following address:

The Globe Pequot Press
Reader Response/Editorial Department
P.O. Box 833
Old Saybrook, CT 06475

Or you may e-mail us at:

editorial@globe-pequot.com

Thanks for your input, and happy travels!

Three Oaks
Bicycle Museum Tour

Number of miles:	19.5 (9.2 for shorter loop)
Approximate pedaling time:	3 hours
Terrain:	Rolling hills
Traffic:	Light
Things to see:	Bicycle Museum, Lake Michigan shoreline, railroad roundhouse, town of New Buffalo
Food:	Many options for food in Three Oaks, New Buffalo, and midway at the Antique Mall and Village in Union Pier

This ride is part of the Backroads Bikeway system, developed and maintained by the Three Oaks Spokes Bicycle Club. The system has twelve diverse loops, all beginning in Three Oaks and all featuring directional signs along the way. The Spokes has done an incredible job of developing the area for bikers. The bike club also maintains the Bicycle Museum/Information Center, the starting point of all the rides. Admission is free, but donations are accepted. It's open from 9:00 A.M. to 5:00 P.M. but closed major holidays and some weekdays. Call (616) 756–3361 to confirm hours.

Housed in the beautiful, old brick depot in downtown Three Oaks, the museum's walls are filled with old advertisements for bicycles and informational panels on the history of bikes. It offers an impressive array of old bikes, such as the Columbia Chainless, circa 1899, and the Ordinary, circa 1880s. The latter is an example of a "highwheeler," with the large front wheel. There's also a "Boneshaker," circa 1860s, that has an all-wood wheel.

Be sure to go behind the depot/museum, across the railroad tracks, to see the Dewey Cannon. This cannon was captured in the

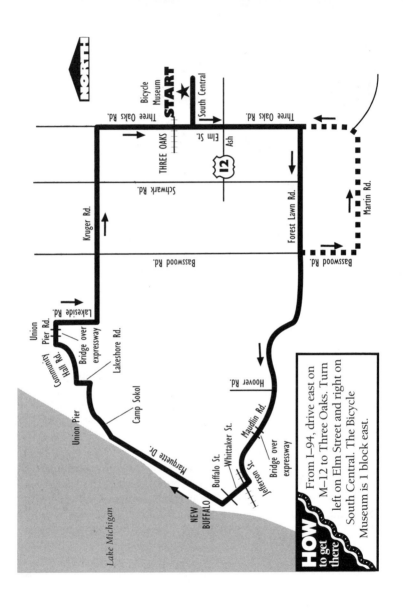

DIRECTIONS at a glance

0.0	From corner of Elm Street and South Central, ride south on Elm. Go straight across U.S. 12 (Ash) at stoplight.
1.6	Turn right onto Forest Lawn Road (watch for bike-chasing—not biting—dog at 2.4 miles).
3.6	Straight after four-way stop at Basswood Road. (Shorter option turns left here.)

4.7 Straight across Lakeside Road. Forest Lawn becomes Maudlin Road.

6.0 Straight at Hoover Road.

7.3 Bridge over expressway.

8.0 Road winds left and becomes Jefferson Street.

8.6 Road dead-ends. Turn right onto Whittaker Street.

8.7 Railroad tracks.

9.1 Straight through stoplight at Buffalo Street.

9.3 Railroad tracks.

9.5 Road curves to right and becomes Marquette Drive.

11.1 Walk bike through gate at Camp Sokol.

12.2 Turn left onto Lakeshore Road.

12.5 Turn right onto Community Hall Road.

12.6 Straight after stop sign at Red Arrow Highway.

12.8 Railroad tracks.

13.9 Turn right onto Union Pier Road.

14.7 Turn right at four-way stop onto Lakeside Road.

15.7 Turn left onto Kruger Road.

16.7 Straight through after stop sign at Basswood Road.

17.7 Straight through intersection with Schwark Road.

18.7 Turn right at stop sign onto Three Oaks Road. Riding into Three Oaks, the road name changes to Elm Street.

19.5 Cross railroad tracks and turn left immediately onto South Central and return to Bicycle Museum.

9.2 miles

0.0 From the corner of Elm Street and South Central, ride south on Elm. Follow longer ride to the corner of Forest Lawn Road and Basswood Road.

3.6 Turn left onto Basswood Road at four-way stop.

4.6 Turn left onto Martin Road.

7.5 Turn left onto Three Oaks Road. (Three Oaks curves at Martin Road, so you almost go straight onto Three Oaks.)

9.1 Straight across U.S. 12 (Ash) at stoplight.

9.2 Turn right onto South Central to return to Bicycle Museum.

Spanish–American War by Admiral George Dewey. It was given to Three Oaks as a token of appreciation of the town's money-raising efforts for a memorial to the men lost on the *Maine*. The park was dedicated by President William McKinley on October 17, 1899, and the cannon on June 28, 1900.

Leaving the museum and riding south out of town, the route moves from residential to rural on good paved roads with low and slow traffic. Because of the Backroads Bikeway, motorists have become very aware of bicycles on the roads and always seem to keep an eye out for them.

In the vicinity of Forest Lawn Road, you'll be amazed at the flashes of yellow you'll see as finches bob and weave in the air in front of you. Forest Lawn actually has its own cemetery, at 2.0 miles. The rest of the road has curves and rolling hills as you make your way among trees.

At 8.6 miles, the road (now Jefferson) ends; across Whittaker Street is The Roundhouse, and behind it is the actual structure where the locomotives were turned around. Also across Whittaker is a tourist information center in an old depot building.

Turn right, cross the railroad tracks, and the New Buffalo watertower looms on the left as you ride into town. Riding through New Buffalo, you'll notice cute shops and restaurants on either side. A picturesque marina is on the left as you ride up a hill at the end of town. At 9.5 miles, the road curves right and becomes Marquette Drive. This section is incredible, with its beautiful dune grasses and expensive homes. The quiet road has trees on the right and glimpses of Lake Michigan on the left.

The public road ends at 11.1 miles, but walk your bike through the gate at Camp Sokol and then continue past camp buildings and houses. Leaving Lake Michigan behind, the route offers trees and fields. At 14.2 miles is an antiques mall, on the right, where food can be enjoyed on the patio. Just 0.1 mile later is a St. Julien Winery tasting center.

At 14.7 miles, turn right onto Lakeside Road. A beautiful tree canopy and downhill follow. A mile later ride uphill to the left turn onto Kruger Road. The ups and downs continue to Schwark Road. Continue straight through the intersection, and the trees fall back from the road and the ride flattens out. To conclude the ride, turn right at 18.7 miles and cruise back into Three Oaks, past older homes down a quaint, tree-lined street.

For a shorter ride, follow the longer ride to the intersection of Basswood Road and turn left. Another left on Martin Road returns you to Three Oaks Road. The shorter option has the same wonderful finches and trees, but it also has a creek at 4.7 miles and another at 7.5 miles. This loop passes marshland filled with wildflowers at 5.4 miles.

THE MAGIC CAPITOL OF THE WORLD

Welcome To

EST 1832

COLON

MAGIC WEEK

AUG. 3 6

The Magical Mystery Tour

Number of miles:	21.4
Approximate pedaling time:	3 hours
Terrain:	Mostly flat
Traffic:	Can be busy in the city of Colon
Things to see:	The "magic capital of the world," Amish farms, lakeshore, wooded rolling hills
Food:	Restaurants and convenience stores in Nottawa and Colon

Sure, the travel brochures may say "Magical Michigan," but in Colon it's no exaggeration. Harry Blackstone, one of the country's most famous and revered magicians in his time, had his home in Colon, where he rested from performing and took time to work on his act.

Fellow magician Percy Abbott came to visit Blackstone in Colon, and he too put down roots here. The two made plans to work together, but after a falling out, it was Abbott's Magic Manufacturing Company, begun in 1933, that eventually became the world's largest maker and supplier of magical accoutrements. It's still supplying magicians the world over. You'll see it on this ride along with the town billed as the "magic capital of the world."

Begin at the Nottawa Park and Public Access, which features drinking water, public rest rooms, picnic tables, and swimming. Leave the park and ride a narrow road with cattail-filled marshes on both sides of the road. At 0.6 mile, the road widens and passes Sand Lake as you journey south on a flat stretch of Nottawa. You'll soon see the shoreline of Lake Templene, also. From lakes, it's on to farmland in the rolling hills of Findley. As you ride into a residential sec-

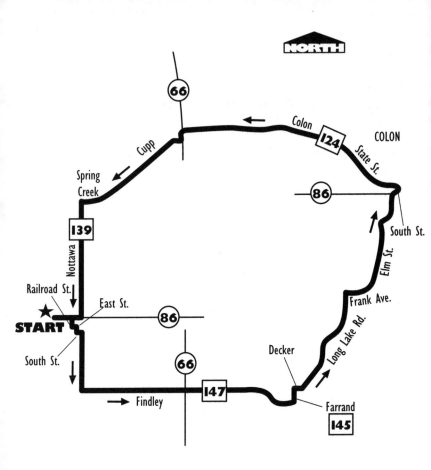

NORTH

66

Colon 124

COLON

Cupp

State St.

Spring
Creek

86

139

South St.

Nottawa

Elm St.

Railroad St.

Frank Ave.

East St.

86

START

Long Lake Rd.

South St.

Decker

66

147

Findley

Farrand

145

HOW to get there — From Business U.S. 131 in Three Rivers, drive east on M–86 to Nottawa. Turn right onto Railroad Street to Nottawa Park and Public Access.

DIRECTIONS at a glance

0.0	Leave park by turning right onto East Street and a quick left onto South Street, the only stretch on gravel roads. At stop sign, turn right onto Nottawa.
1.2	Turn left onto Findley, County Road 147.
3.2	Continue straight after stop sign at M–66.

4.8 Series of tight curves. (*Caution:* Ride far enough out in lane so drivers can see you as they round the corner.)

5.5 Turn left onto Farrand, County Road 145.

8.2 Turn right onto Decker.

8.8 Veer left at Y (Long Lake Road, no street sign) so that the marsh is on your right.

10.2 Road curves right and becomes Frank Avenue; it soon curves to the left and becomes Elm Street.

11.0 Turn right onto South Street into the town of Colon.

11.2 Four-way stop. Turn left onto State Street (business district to the right). First street on the left is St. Joseph, with Abbott's Magic Company on right side of street. Continue straight on State Street, which becomes Colon, County Road 124.

16.0 Stop sign at M–66. Cross road and turn left.

16.1 Turn right onto Cupp, the first street on right.

18.2 Stop and turn right onto Spring Creek.

18.6 Stop and turn left onto Nottawa, County Road 139.

21.1 Stop and turn right onto M–86.

21.2 Turn left onto Railroad Street.

21.4 Enter park.

tion at 4.8 miles, *use caution* on a series of tight curves—make sure drivers can see you.

A left on Farrand at 5.5 miles offers woods on both sides of the road. Then, after turns on Decker and Long Lake Road, the view changes again to lakes. You'll still see lakes as you move into the quiet residential section of Colon. Be sure to look up and left at the curve onto Frank Avenue to see the Colon watertower.

After a steep hill on South Street, you'll be rewarded with downtown Colon. Don't miss the flower containers that line State Street. A look under the greenery reveals big black top hats, used upside-down as flower planters. Explore the shops to the right or make a left and ride a block to St. Joseph Street and Abbott's Magic Company.

Inside Abbott's unassuming cement-block building (which is as innocent as the proverbial top hat) are photographs of some of the famous magicians who have connections to Abbott's and its wares. A display room lets you see thousands of tricks, but not their secrets, although once you make a purchase, all secrets will be revealed by one of the crafty workers.

Abbott's and Colon host more than a thousand people each year in August at the Magical Get-Together. Professionals, amateurs, and aficionados talk magic and compare their arts during lectures, close-up shows, talent contests, and a benefit matinee.

Leaving town, the busy stretch on Colon soon gives way to a quieter road lined with farms. Keep an eye out for Amish buggies. Rolling hills, trees, and wildflowers lead you back to Nottawa. On Nottawa, you'll see the huge but elegant draft horses that the Amish use for farmwork, grazing in the fields or standing patiently near the barns. Turn off Nottawa and you'll return to the cool trees and water of the park.

It's a Grrrreat Ride!:
Battle Creek

Number of miles:	10.4 (6.7 for shorter loop)
Approximate pedaling time:	90 minutes
Terrain:	Mostly flat
Traffic:	Some very busy intersections when trail crosses roads
Things to see:	Riverfront Park, Kalamazoo and Battle Creek Rivers, the Underground Railroad sculpture
Food:	Many places for food downtown and along Capital Avenue from 3.2 miles to 3.6 miles

Tony the Tiger lives here as well as Snap, Crackle, and Pop. You won't see them on the ride, but you will see evidence of their bosses. Known as "Cereal City" or the "Breakfast Capital of the World," Battle Creek is home not only to Kellogg and Post but also to a great linear park.

The paved Battle Creek Linear Park passes through the city, runs along water and woods, and is so well marked that you cannot lose your way. It begins in the Downtown Riverfront Park, located on both sides of the Battle Creek River. The park features old-fashioned street-lights and colored bricks laid in interesting patterns. There are benches and bridges to use for different views of the river as it meanders through the downtown park.

The linear park offers many options for bicyclists: a perimeter loop of 10.4 miles, which is featured here and marked along the path by purple signs; a west loop of 7.1 miles, marked with blue signs; an east loop of 6.7 miles, marked along the path by red signs; and two non-loop paths, which run on either side of the Kalamazoo River to

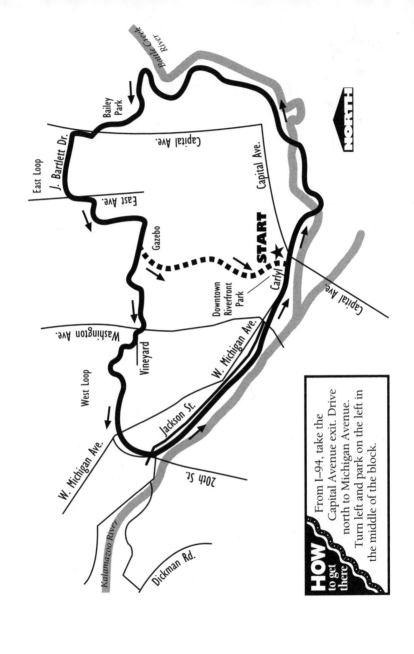

NORTH

Battle Creek River

Bailey Park

East Loop

J. Bartlett Dr.

Capital Ave.

East Ave.

Gazebo

Capital Ave.

START

Carlyl

Capital Ave.

Downtown Riverfront Park

Washington Ave.

Vineyard

W. Michigan Ave.

West Loop

Jackson St.

W. Michigan Ave.

20th St.

Kalamazoo River

Dickman Rd.

HOW to get there

From I-94, take the Capital Avenue exit. Drive north to Michigan Avenue. Turn left and park on the left in the middle of the block.

DIRECTIONS at a glance

Note: Follow directions carefully, as not every small street is shown on the map.

0.0 Leaving parking lot, walk bike across West Michigan Avenue to reach the Downtown Riverfront Park.

0.1 Cross the river and turn right.

0.2 Cross Capital Avenue.

0.4 Cross street and continue straight.

0.7 Stop and continue straight.

1.0 Cross street and ride sidewalk to cross bridge.

1.1 Sharp right after crossing bridge.

1.6 Playground and scenic overlook on right.

2.0 Trail veers right, leaves road, and goes into trees.

2.3 Veer right as path moves toward river and under Emmett Street.

2.8 Path swings left. Yield to traffic while crossing two roads.

3.0 Stop and cross Roosevelt Avenue to enter Bailey Park.

3.2 Two stop signs to cross road entrance to Bailey Park. Path then turns across Capital Avenue. (*Caution:* Watch out for traffic at business entrances.)

3.4 Turn left at J. Bartlett Drive.

3.5 Yield to traffic and take sharp right to cross J. Bartlett Drive to follow path.

3.7 Turn left on East Avenue, crossing J. Bartlett Drive.

4.0 Trail crosses street.

4.1 Four-way stop at East Avenue and Russell. Continue straight.

4.3 Curve right as trail leaves road and goes through field.

4.6 Yield to traffic and cross street.

4.7 Veer right on trail. Path to left goes to gazebo loop.

4.9 Gazebo path joins main trail again.

5.0 Trail has T. To left is downtown. The shorter loop turns here. Turn right for longer loop.

5.1 Stop and cross road. Trail swings left and climbs hill. (*Caution:* Stop sign on downhill run.)

5.4 Stop and cross North Avenue.

5.5 Cross Roosevelt Avenue and make sharp left.

5.9 Stop for traffic and cross Washington Avenue. Turn right onto Washington and then left onto Vineyard.

6.2 Turn right to go downhill and then turn left.

6.4 Yield to traffic and turn right to cross street.

6.6 Four-way stop. Cross Hubbard Street and turn left to cross Goodale Avenue.

7.0 Veer right. Path on left goes to parking lot.

7.3 Veer right.

7.4 Stop and cross street.

7.7 Cross West Michigan Avenue at light.

7.9 Cross Jackson Street and make a sharp left to ride back along river. Turn right at this intersection to leave loop and follow river farther west.

9.2 Stop and cross Angell Street.

9.8 Stop and cross Washington Avenue. Turn left and ride north.

10.0 Turn right onto West Michigan Avenue.

10.4 Enter downtown. Turn right and retrace steps to parking lot.

6.7 miles

Follow directions for longer loop until 5.0 miles.

5.0 Turn left at T. Follow path across North Avenue, Emmett Street, and Van Buren Street.

6.7 Enter Downtown Riverfront Park. Turn left and retrace steps to parking lot.

---

the west of Twentieth Street and the perimeter loop. The 3.6-mile non-loop ride from Twentieth Street to Dickman Road is especially scenic and a great addition to the perimeter loop.

Leaving the park heading east, just after crossing Capital Avenue, the W. K. Kellogg Foundation headquarters is on your right. Its financial support helped make the linear park possible. Winding among flower beds and small hills, the path next passes the Underground Railroad sculpture, created by Ed Dwight. The sculpture honors

slaves who fled north and the people who helped them obtain their freedom on the Underground Railroad. It may seem like a strange location for the sculpture, but on the other side of the Battle Creek River lived Erastus and Sarah Hussey, "conductors" on the railroad who helped more than 1,000 people reach safety in the north.

Leaving downtown, the path continues alongside the Battle Creek River. This section is especially beautiful, with plenty of trees, ponds, and wildflowers. There are just enough hills and curves to keep the ride interesting but not too challenging. At 2.3 miles, don't miss the small waterfall.

Half a mile later, the path runs alongside busy Capital Avenue. There are plenty of fast-food places and supermarkets on the west side of Capital Avenue; and on the other side is Bailey Park.

Turning west away from the commercial area at 3.6 miles, the path returns to quiet residential streets. Then it passes through a large field and across a wooden bridge at 4.6 miles. Less than a mile later is the junction or midsection of the perimeter loop. Turn left to take the shorter option loop or right to continue the longer loop.

By 7.9 miles, the path begins its journey east along a beautiful stretch of the Kalamazoo River. At Jackson Street, the perimeter loop is the path to the left. The path to the right runs to Dickman Road, where it ends. The perimeter route is quiet as it works toward downtown between the Kalamazoo River and the backyards of houses. At Washington Avenue, turn left to ride to West Michigan Avenue. Continue on West Michigan Avenue until you regain the river at Downtown Riverfront Park. A great place to eat after the ride is Clara's, located in a Michigan Central Railroad depot, built in 1888.

I Got a Ride in Kalamazoo:
Kal-Haven Trail State Park

Number of miles:	29.8 (shorter option to ride trail and return by same route)
Approximate pedaling time:	4½ hours
Terrain:	First half flat, second half killer hills
Traffic:	Heavy bicycle traffic on holiday weekends on trail; light traffic on roads
Things to see:	Kal-Haven Trail Sesquicentennial State Park, small towns of Alamo, Kendall, and Gobles
Food:	Alamo, Kendall, Beehive Farm Market, Gobles

This ride begins on the Kalamazoo side of the Kal-Haven Sesquicentennial Trail State Park (see Ride 5 for South Haven Side Ride). This is another fine job done by Michigan's Rails-to-Trails Conservancy and the Department of Natural Resources. Running between Kalamazoo and South Haven on an abandoned rail corridor, this 34-mile path of crushed limestone opened in 1989 and has been immensely popular. The first half of the ride, on the trail, is easygoing. The second half, on roads, is not recommended for the faint of knee.

They couldn't have designed a better way to begin the trail. From the parking lot ride up a small ramp to a red caboose. A head pops out of the window to ask if you want a daily or an annual pass. Continue down the ramp as it swings onto the trail.

The trail features caution signs for driveways and stop signs at street crossings. Oasis signs dot the trail, announcing which towns have food available. Besides signs, along the trail are chipmunks and groundhogs, pit toilets and picnic tables, marshes, creeks, bridges, wildflowers, and plenty of trees.

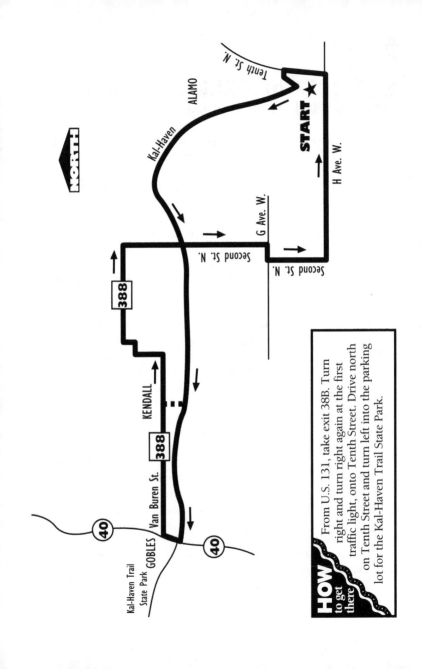

NORTH

Tenth St. N.

ALAMO

Kal-Haven

START

H Ave. W.

G Ave. W.

Second St. N.

Second St. N.

388

KENDALL

388

Van Buren St.

40

GOBLES

40

Kal-Haven Trail
State Park

HOW to get there

From U.S. 131, take exit 38B. Turn
right and turn right again at the first
traffic light, onto Tenth Street. Drive north
on Tenth Street and turn left into the parking
lot for the Kal-Haven Trail State Park.

DIREC-TIONS at a glance

Note: This trail contains many crossroads and driveways, which are not noted in these directions. Follow trail signs.

0.0   Ride bike up to caboose to purchase trail pass. Continue down ramp, which leads to trail. Veer right.

0.7   Stop at unmarked crossroad and continue straight.

2.7   Stop and cross Owen Drive. Then cross several driveways.

2.9   Stop and continue straight. Village of Alamo can be seen down this road to the right.

9.7   Stop and cross road. Village of Kendall can be seen down to the right.

13.2   Stop and turn right onto M–40, heading toward the town of Gobles.

13.4   Turn right onto Van Buren Street, CR 388.

16.5   Enter Kendall.

17.2   Continue straight at intersection with CR 653 to right, and Twenty-sixth Street to left.

21.1   Turn right onto Second Street N.

22.3   Cross Kal-Haven Trail.

24.1   Stop at G Avenue W., and jog right and then left to continue on Second Street N.

25.1   Turn left onto H Avenue W.

25.6   Stop and cross Third Street N.

27.1   Stop and cross Sixth Street N.

28.4   Stop and cross Ninth Street N.

29.1   Stop and turn left onto Tenth Street N.

29.7   Turn left into parking lot.

29.8   Return to parking lot.

Curve left at 1.0 mile, and ride by tall trees before crossing a bridge at 1.6 miles. The vegetation thins at 1.9 miles, followed 0.4 mile later with a swamp. The mostly flat trail continues to switch from lush green trees and ferns to wide-open blue sky.

The village of Alamo appears at 2.9 miles. Swing right off the trail for food or drink. At 8.5 miles, following a stop, enjoy a long, gentle uphill with a final steep bank up to the stop sign at 9.1 miles. Cross the road and coast down the steep hill. High banks on both sides of the trail make it seem like a tunnel. The banks quickly fall away, and the trail rides high above the surrounding land as if on a platform.

Pass Kendall at 9.7 miles, or stop for snacks. Then it's into Gobles at 13.2 miles. Turn right and ride north through town on M–40's wide lanes. Turn right again on CO 388. At 14.1 miles, Gobles Recreational Park offers picnic tables, drinking water, and rest rooms. There are plenty of places for breaks in the next section: at 15.1 miles, a fruit stand; and 16.7 miles, a country store.

Cruise into Kendall, at 16.5 miles, with its picturesque post office and church. Then you can see a hill coming, and it won't be the first or biggest. At 17.7 miles start a great downhill and curve hard left, only to begin an uphill that lasts until 18.2 miles. (Cherry Hill Farm is here, along with a great view of the surrounding area.)

Curve right at the pond with lily pads and begin a big uphill at 18.6 miles. Be cautious on the way down, as gravel takes up most of the shoulder. Turn right onto Second Street North at 21.1 miles. Enjoy a respite from huge hills. At 24.1 miles, jog right to keep on Second Street North.

A long uphill leads to the stop sign at G Avenue West. Ride another big up-and-down before turning left, at 25.1 miles, onto H Avenue West. Here the hills get serious. You'll see more tops and bottoms of trees than a gray squirrel—but think of those thighs!

Turn left onto Tenth Street North and hold on. One more down-and-up and it's into the parking lot, at 29.8 miles.

South Haven Side Ride

Number of miles:	13.6
Approximate pedaling time:	90 minutes
Terrain:	Mostly flat
Traffic:	Light
Things to see:	Kal-Haven Trail Sesquicentennial Park, Black River, fields and farms
Food:	Pop and ice-cream stand at Kibbie

This is another ride made possible by the wonderful work of Michigan's Rails-to-Trails Conservancy and the Department of Natural Resources. In 1987 the DNR bought 433 acres of abandoned rail corridor between South Haven and Kalamazoo, with plans to open the linear park in time for the state's 150th birthday, hence the Sesquicentennial Park moniker. Even though it took until 1989 to open, the result was well worth the wait. The 34-mile path of crushed limestone is a jewel in the state park system's crown, according to the thousands of bikers, hikers, horseback riders, cross-country skiers, and snowmobilers who have enjoyed its vistas of woods, farms, grasslands, and wetlands.

Land has already been purchased to extend the trail to the South Haven Pier, but until then this ride begins at the current trail end, at the Black River and Blue Star Highway. It's a great family ride if you take the trail and return on it—there is no street traffic, and a plethora of signs warn of stops and driveways. For the more adventurous, the second half of the ride continues off the trail into the heart of blueberry country.

Walk your bike out of the parking area down a small hill, and you'll encounter a small kiosk where trail passes are sold. For a nomi-

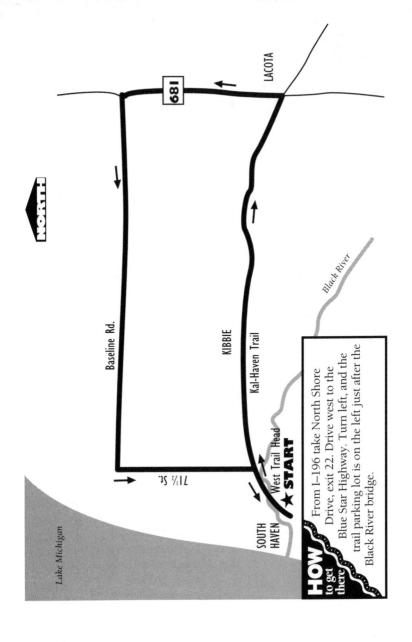

NORTH

LACOTA

189

Baseline Rd.

71½ St.

Lake Michigan

SOUTH HAVEN

West Trail Head
★ START

KIBBIE

Kal-Haven Trail

Black River

HOW to get there

From I-196 take North Shore Drive, exit 22. Drive west to the Blue Star Highway. Turn left, and the trail parking lot is on the left just after the Black River bridge.

DIREC-TIONS at a glance

0.0	From parking lot, walk your bike down the hill to the kiosk to buy your pass.
0.9	Continue straight after stop sign.
1.6	Continue straight after stop sign.
2.6	Continue straight after stop sign.
3.1	Continue straight after stop sign.
3.5	Continue straight after stop sign.
4.6	Continue straight after stop sign.
6.6	Turn left (north) at stop sign at Lacota onto County Road 681.
7.0	Turn left onto Baseline Road as County Road 681 begins to turn right.
8.2	Cross Sixty-second Street.
8.5	Cross Sixty-third Street.
9.0	Pavement begins.
10.0	Stop and continue straight across County Road 687, Sixty-sixth Street.
11.0	Cross Sixty-eighth Street.
12.7	Turn left off Baseline Road onto 71½ Street. Immediately turn right to regain trail.
13.6	Return to trail's end.

nal fee, you may buy a daily or an annual pass. Hop onto your bike and enjoy the first part of the tree-lined trail that follows the beautiful Black River. Along the trail, you'll find benches where you can sit and rest or just stop and admire the view. The first great place to stop is the Nichols Covered Bridge, at 0.3 mile. The trail rides over the bridge, built by the Civilian Conservation Corps in 1988 and named in memory of Donald F. Nichols, whose family donated the materials.

The packed, crushed limestone/slag is fast-going, but take care to avoid the edges of the trail, where occasionally there are piles of gravel that make for tricky and sloppy riding. Also, watch for the signs warning of stops and driveways. By 3.3 miles, you'll see a sign for the junction of Kibbie. A backyard entrepreneur has set up a pop and ice-cream stand here. Farther on, between Kibbie and Lacota, the trees give way to fields and farms. At 6.6 miles, you'll cruise into Lacota. Here, the ride leaves the trail and turns left onto County Road 681, passing the homes in sleepy Lacota.

The second half of the ride alternates between trees and fields. As you reach the bottom of a hill at 7.0 miles, *watch out* for gravel. Here's where you turn onto Baseline Road, a well-maintained gravel road that actually rides faster than the trail. At 8.4 miles, you're joined by guinea hens running by and across the road, with their beautiful black-and-white–spotted feathers. Pavement begins again at 9.0 miles.

Less than 2 miles later, you'll pass on the right one of the area's many fruit stands and "U-Pick" places for blueberries. The ride leaves the farms and once again moves through trees that line the road. Then a left and a quick right bring you back to the trail and another look at the beautiful covered bridge over the Black River.

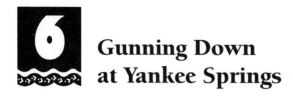

Gunning Down
at Yankee Springs

Number of miles:	14.7
Approximate pedaling time:	2 hours
Terrain:	Hills, then flat
Traffic:	Light
Things to see:	Gun Lake, Yankee Springs Recreational Area, Allegan County Park, woods and wildflowers
Food:	Available frequently along route except between 0.3 and 7.6 miles

Ride through some of the 5,000 acres filled with bogs, marshes, lakes, streams, and nature trails at Yankee Springs Recreational Area as this route travels around Gun Lake. The loop shows both the wild east side of the Gun Lake area and the developed west side; at times you're riding so close to the water on either side that you could reach out a foot and put your toes in Gun Lake.

Ride out of the Gun Lake Unit of the recreational area, turning right onto Gun Lake Road, to enjoy wide, paved shoulders with trees on both sides and the lake, sometimes only a few feet away. Some stretches of the shoulder have gravel, so use caution. At 0.3 mile, there are stores and restaurants; a curve and a hill later, the route is back between lake and trees. This section has some good-sized hills, but there usually is a downhill for every uphill.

The shoulder disappears on Yankee Springs Road, but traffic generally moves slowly through its curves. Beautiful wildflowers line the road here. The shoulder returns on Wildwood Road. There is a great downhill at 5.9 miles, but be careful of gravel at the bottom as the road curves left. The last big hill is at 6.5 miles, and then the route flattens.

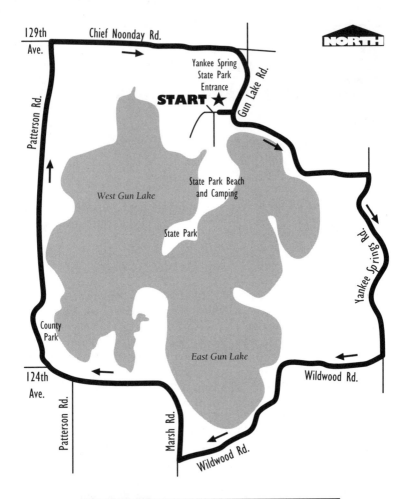

129th Ave.

Chief Noonday Rd.

Yankee Spring State Park Entrance

START ★

Gun Lake Rd.

Patterson Rd.

West Gun Lake

State Park Beach and Camping

State Park

Yankee Springs Rd.

County Park

124th Ave.

East Gun Lake

Patterson Rd.

Marsh Rd.

Wildwood Rd.

Wildwood Rd.

NORTH

HOW to get there From U.S. 131, take exit 61, Hopkins/Bradley. Drive east until the Y, and then veer right onto Gun Lake Road. The entrance to the Gun Lake Unit is the second driveway on the right.

DIREC-TIONS at a glance

0.0	Turn right out of Gun Lake Unit entrance onto Gun Lake Road.
3.0	Turn right at stop sign at Yankee Springs Road.
4.2	Turn right onto Wildwood Road.
5.9	Begin downhill run. (*Caution:* Gravel on shoulder at bottom of hill.)
7.3	Stop and turn right onto Marsh Road.
9.3	Cross county line; Marsh Road becomes Patterson Road.
9.7	Patterson Road curves right at intersection with 124th Avenue.
12.3	Turn right at four-way stop onto Chief Noonday Road.
13.8	Stay on shoulder as it veers right onto Gun Lake Road.
14.7	Turn right into Gun Lake Unit.

Just after the turn onto the wonderful wide shoulder of Marsh Road, the scenery changes from trees to lake. This section is filled with marinas, boat docks, and lake views on the right, shops and restaurants on the left. Curve away from the lake at 8.3 miles, and pass a farm market 0.3 mile later, on the left.

Marsh Road becomes Patterson Road at 9.3 miles as the loop leaves one county and enters the next. The road here is wide and traffic moves slowly. As the road curves right, it passes Allegan County Park, a good place for a break, providing beach access, rest rooms, drinking water, picnic tables, and shade. Water and rest rooms are on the west side of the road. There are also a pharmacy and grocery store.

Farther down Patterson Road is Daisy Mae's Tavern, on the left. A flat stretch on Patterson leads to Chief Noonday Road, where food and drink are available. Chief Noonday, the namesake of both the road and a trail in the area, was an Ottawa Indian chief who lived in the Yankee Springs area. The road is heavily traveled, but the wide, paved shoulder allows so much room between bicycles and cars that the traffic is not a bother.

Veer right at 13.8 miles, following the shoulder onto Gun Lake Road. Less than a mile is the entrance to the state park.

The Saugatuck Sashay

Number of miles:	29.5 (23.1 miles for shorter option)
Approximate pedaling time:	4 hours
Terrain:	Rolling hills
Traffic:	Can be heavy on Fifty-eighth Street
Things to see:	Towns of Saugatuck, Fennville, and Douglas, Hutchins Lake, Fenn Valley Vineyards, Kalamazoo River
Food:	Saugatuck, Fennville, Douglas

Divided by the Kalamazoo River, the tourist towns of Saugatuck and Douglas, located on the Lake Michigan coastline, have for years attracted crowds, especially from Chicago, via trains, boats, and autos. Formerly a large artists' colony, the towns charm visitors with trendy boutiques, galleries and art shows, diverse restaurants, and lake views from atop high, white sandy dunes.

During this ride it becomes apparent why the area is so popular. Along with the towns, you'll experience rolling hills through hardwoods and pines, fields and wildflowers, one of Michigan's best wineries, and views of Hutchins Lake and the Kalamazoo River. Begin north of Saugatuck's shops, at the intersection of Butler and Main Streets, where there are parks on either side of the road. The park to the east offers drinking water and rest rooms.

You'll ride roads north out of Saugatuck as the route turns and twists past elegant homes. Wide shoulders lead past the Saugatuck Dunes State Park, at 3.6 miles—it's a fun place to get sand in your shoes climbing dunes that tower 180 feet above Lake Michigan. The park has picnic tables, hiking trails, and rest rooms.

Continue over rolling hills covered with pines and wildflowers. At

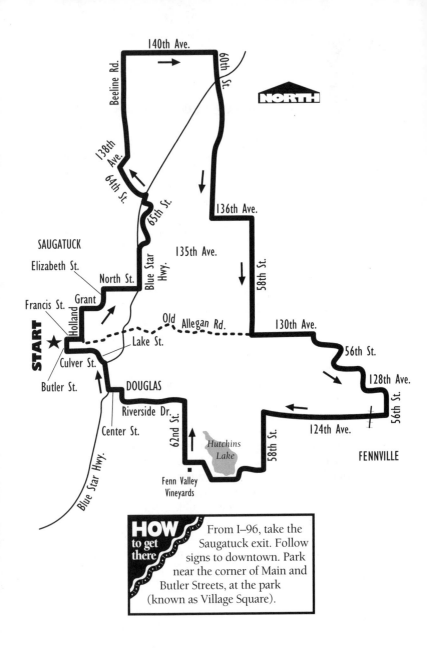

140th Ave.

60th St.

Beeline Rd.

NORTH

138th Ave.

64th St.

65th St.

136th Ave.

SAUGATUCK

135th Ave.

Blue Star Hwy.

58th St.

Elizabeth St.

North St.

Francis St.

Grant

Holland

Old Allegan Rd.

130th Ave.

START

Lake St.

56th St.

Culver St.

128th Ave.

Butler St.

DOUGLAS

56th St.

Riverside Dr.

124th Ave.

Center St.

62nd St.

Hutchins Lake

58th St.

FENNVILLE

Blue Star Hwy.

Fenn Valley Vineyards

HOW to get there — From I–96, take the Saugatuck exit. Follow signs to downtown. Park near the corner of Main and Butler Streets, at the park (known as Village Square).

DIREC-TIONS at a glance

0.0	Ride north on Butler Street.
0.1	At four-way stop, turn right onto Francis Street.
0.15	At three-way stop, turn left onto Holland.
0.5	Turn right onto Grant. Road curves left and becomes Elizabeth Street.

0.7 Stop and turn right onto North Street.

1.0 Stop and turn left onto Blue Star Highway.

1.9 Turn right onto 135th Avenue. Road curves right and becomes Sixty-fifth Street.

2.5 Stop and turn right onto Blue Star Highway.

2.6 Turn left onto Sixty-fourth Street.

3.6 Turn right onto 138th Avenue. Road curves left and becomes Beeline Road.

4.8 Stop and turn right onto 140th Avenue.

6.5 Stop and turn right onto Sixtieth Street.

7.6 Stop and continue straight across Blue Star Highway.

8.5 Stop and turn left onto 136th Avenue.

9.6 Stop and turn right onto Fifty-eighth Street.

12.9 Turn left onto 130th Avenue.

13.5 Stop and turn right onto Fifty-seventh Street.

13.8 Curve right and road becomes Fifty-sixth Street.

14.5 Curve left and road becomes 128th Avenue.

14.7 Curve right and road becomes Fifty-sixth Street.

16.2 Enter Fennville city limits.

16.3 Railroad crossing.

16.7 Turn right onto 124th Avenue into Fennville.

17.1 Railroad crossing. Road becomes Main Street.

17.7 Turn left onto Fifty-eighth Street as you leave town.

19.0 Curve right. Road becomes 122nd Avenue.

19.3 Hutchins Lake.

21.1 Turn right onto Sixty-second Street.

22.2 Stop and cross M–89.

24.8 Curve left. Road becomes Riverside Drive.

27.0   After riding over expressway, turn right onto Water Street.

27.6   Curve left. Road becomes Center Street. Enter Douglas.

27.7   Continue straight after four-way stop at Main Street.

28.0   Turn right onto Blue Star Highway.

28.7   Turn left onto Lake Street, which becomes Culver Street.

29.3   Continue straight at four-way stop at Griffith Street. Turn right onto Butler Street.

29.5   Return to Village Square.

23.1 miles

0.0   Ride north on Butler Street.

0.1   At four-way stop, turn right onto Francis Street.

0.15   At three-way stop, continue straight.

0.4   Curve right onto Elizabeth Street.

0.7   Stop and turn left onto Allegan Street.

1.1   Stop and continue straight across Blue Star Highway. Road becomes Old Allegan Road.

5.3   Stop and turn right onto Fifty-eighth Street, rejoining longer loop. Return to park at 23.1 miles.

9.6 miles, turn right onto Fifty-eighth Street, where traffic can be heavy. The shoulder widens during a great downhill to a view of the river at 12.2 miles. Curves and an uphill then lead to the turn onto 130th Avenue. You'll lose the hills but keep the trees and curves here. At 13.5 miles, stop and turn right onto Fifty-seventh Street. Turn left here for a quick side trip to the small village of New Richmond and its great, old church.

Move into an area where every curve means a change in the road's name. At 16.7 miles, turn right onto 124th Avenue into Fennville, home of the Goose Festival every October. Canada geese flock to the area, and their visit is commemorated with goose calling, the Wild Goose Chase run, and other activities.

After Fennville, ride south toward Hutchins Lake where 122nd Avenue hugs the southern and southwestern lakeshore. Turn left away from the lake, and pass rows of vines before reaching Fenn Valley Vineyards at 20.5 miles. The winery offers self-guided tours and tastings of its many superb wines and champagnes. More vineyards and orchards border the road as the rolling hills continue.

Some of the fruit that you see growing on the route is for sale at the fruit stand at the intersection with M–89, at 22.2 miles. Enjoy an easy stretch of straight flatland before curving left onto Riverside Drive, where the Kalamazoo River makes a blue backdrop for the trees. Cross a creek at 25.9 miles before riding up and over the expressway. On the way down, be ready for the right turn onto Water Street. Several curves later, ride into downtown Douglas, with its shops and restaurants.

Follow the Blue Star Highway across the Kalamazoo River. Look left for a great view of boats bobbing on the water, to the right for the winding, grassy banks of the Kalamazoo. Just after crossing the bridge, turn left onto Lake Street, which becomes Culver Street. At 29.3 miles turn right onto Butler Street.

Heavy traffic, both pedestrian and auto, fill this section of Butler Street. Move carefully past the shops, restaurants, delis, ice-cream parlor, and galleries, on the way back to the Village Square at 29.5 miles.

Unlike the longer route, the shorter option heads east out of Saugatuck, on Allegan Street. After crossing the Blue Star Highway, it becomes Old Allegan Road, a narrow tree-lined thoroughfare that follows an old Native American trail. In the 1800s, stagecoaches used the road to travel to Lake Michigan. It's a nice stretch of old trees, curves, and hills. At 5.3 miles, you join the longer ride on Fifty-eighth Street and head toward Fennville, Hutchins Lake, Fenn Valley Vineyards, and finally, picturesque Douglas and Saugatuck.

Tulip City Tour:
Holland

Number of miles:	23.9 (13.7 for shorter loop)
Approximate pedaling time:	3 hours
Terrain:	Mostly flat
Traffic:	Light after congestion at beginning
Things to see:	Lake Michigan, Holland State Park, Lake Macatawa, Tunnel Park
Food:	Cafe at state park. On Ottawa Beach Road: Ottawa Beach Inn, at 0.7 mile; Meyer's Bar-B-Q, 3.4 miles; Side Door Party Store & Deli, 4.4 miles. On River Avenue: 5.9 miles, many fast-food restaurants, at the intersection of Butternut Drive and Lake Shore Drive; 14.3 miles, Sandy Point Restaurant

People around the world flock to Holland in western Michigan during May for the annual Tulip Festival. The tulip is king in this town of Dutch descendants; the bicycle paths are royal, also. Wide asphalt or cement paths parallel busy streets, tree-lined country lanes, and the Lake Michigan coastline. With the wonderful park system, there are plenty of places to stop along the way with scenic vistas, and picnic and rest room facilities.

This ride showcases all the great things the area has to offer, from beach scenes to business districts to quiet, tree-lined country roads. You'll pass the county fairgrounds, three parks, and the Kiwanis rest stop on this mostly flat ride.

Start at Holland State Park, known for its red lighthouse and wide, white-sand Lake Michigan beach. Leaving the park via Ottawa Beach Road, you'll ride along Lake Macatawa and be able to watch

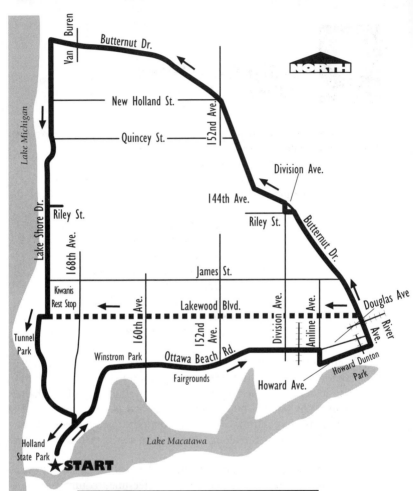

Van Buren

Butternut Dr.

NORTH

New Holland St.

152nd Ave.

Quincey St.

Lake Michigan

Division Ave.

144th Ave.

Lake Shore Dr.

Riley St.

Riley St.

Butternut Dr.

168th Ave.

James St.

Kiwanis Rest Stop

160th Ave.

Lakewood Blvd.

Division Ave.

Aniline Ave.

Douglas Ave

Tunnel Park

152nd Ave.

River Ave.

Winstrom Park

Ottawa Beach Rd.

Howard Dunton Park

Fairgrounds

Howard Ave.

Holland State Park

★ START

Lake Macatawa

HOW to get there Take exit 55 from I–196, and head west toward Holland. Turn right onto 112th Avenue, then left onto Lakewood Boulevard. Veer left onto Douglas Avenue. Douglas turns into Ottawa Beach Road, which dead-ends at Holland State Park.

DIREC-TIONS at a glance

0.0 Leave Holland State Park riding the bicycle path on Ottawa Beach Road.

1.5 Yield at intersection to car traffic.

2.2 Yield to cross traffic at intersection. Win strom Park on left.

3.1 Pass Ottawa County Fairgrounds.

3.3 Traffic light at Kalamazoo.

4.3 Traffic light at Division Avenue.

4.8 Railroad tracks.

4.9 Turn right on Aniline Avenue.

5.0 Stop sign at Howard Avenue. Cross Howard, turn left, and ride sidewalk/bike path.

5.3 Howard B. Dunton Park.

5.6 Railroad tracks.

5.8 Turn left at River Avenue without crossing the street.

5.9 Straight across Douglas Avenue intersection.

6.0 Railroad tracks.

6.1 Straight across Lakewood Boulevard. (Short loop turns left.)

6.3 Stay left on Butternut Drive at Y.

6.7 Straight through intersection at James Street.

8.0 Veer left onto Riley Street as Butternut Drive veers right.

8.1 Four-way stop at 144th Avenue. Cross 144th Avenue and turn right.

8.2 Turn left onto Butternut Drive.

12.2 Cross Van Buren and watch out for cars turning left.

14.3 Veer left on path onto Lake Shore Drive.

14.6 Steep slope.

20.8 Kiwanis rest stop.

21.1 Straight across Lakewood Boulevard and turn right as path moves to west side of Lake Shore Drive. Short loop connects to ride here.

21.5 Tunnel Park.

22.9 Right on 168th Avenue where Lake Shore Drive dead-ends.

23.0 Turn right onto Ottawa Beach Road.

23.9 Holland State Park entrance.

13.7 miles

Follow longer ride until Lakewood Boulevard at 6.1 miles.

6.1 Turn left onto Lakewood Boulevard; go straight for 4.8 miles.

10.9 Turn left onto Lake Shore Drive and follow directions for longer route back to state park (at 21.1 miles).

---

the parade of sailboats and speedboats heading out to or coming in from Lake Michigan. You'll have time to look, as it's slow going because of the many pedestrians and in-line skaters. Traffic on the path quiets down after 168th Street.

Winstrom Park is the next park on the route; it has its own bike path, if you want to turn off and explore. A mile later, the county fairgrounds offer parking and public rest rooms. Also in this area are an antiques shop, a barbecue restaurant, and a supermarket for picnic supplies.

At Division Avenue, Ottawa Beach Road changes its name to Douglas Avenue. Then, after two turns, the bike path becomes a wide sidewalk. This leads to Howard B. Dunton Park, with picnic tables, public rest rooms, and another view of the sailboats crisscrossing Lake Macatawa. A path to the right goes downhill to the lake and ends at a perfect picnic area. Leaving the quiet of the park, a left on River Avenue leads to a business area with many fast-food restaurants. *Use caution* with the driveways.

At 6.1 miles, cross Lakewood Boulevard and continue north. If you are taking the shorter option, though, turn left, and the bike path on Lakewood Boulevard begins after the first parking lot.

At the **Y** in the road, veer left; the route is now on Butternut Drive. At 8.0 miles, a short jog to the left on Riley Street leads to 144th Avenue, where turning north will put you back on Butternut Drive. Just past this jog is Lakeshore Cycle, in case you have any bike problems. In less than a mile, the ride heads out into the country, where the businesses give way to pine trees. *Watch out* at 12.2 miles for cars turning left onto Van Buren from Butternut Drive.

At 14.3 miles, turn south onto Lake Shore Drive. There begins a series of humps, although there is a steep slope at 14.6 miles. Before you do too much work, the ride flattens out and trees form a canopy over the road.

Two more great places to stop: the entrance to the Kiwanis Kamp, where the Kiwanis have created a rest stop with a picnic table and drinking fountain; and Tunnel Park, a local favorite, with sandy beaches, picnic tables, and public rest rooms. Just after the rest stop and before Tunnel Park, the path crosses Lakewood Boulevard, where the shorter-option riders rejoin the loop. Lake Shore Drive dead-ends into 168th Avenue, where a short jog to the right leads to Ottawa Beach Road. Turn right, pass a few in-line skaters, and you're back to beautiful Holland State Park.

The Coast Guard City Tour:
Grand Haven

Number of miles:	13.9 (5.1 for shorter loop, 17.0 for pier extension)
Approximate pedaling time:	2 hours
Terrain:	Mostly flat (pier loop hilly)
Traffic:	Congestion on pier loop on holiday weekends, light on the rest of ride
Things to see:	Lake Michigan, Grand Haven pier and boardwalk, Grand River, Tri-Cities Historical Museum
Food:	Many restaurants and convenience stores toward the beginning and end of ride

To many people, Grand Haven is famous for three things: its Coast Guard Festival in August, with parades and water shows; one of the best Lake Michigan beaches; and its musical fountain—water dancing with music and lights—said to be the world's largest. It should also be famous for its biker-friendly roads.

This route rides on low-traffic roads and bike paths, and along the way you'll see residential areas, parks, and the Grand River. The optional loop rides out on the breathtaking Grand Haven pier for a close look at the famous lighthouse, via the Grand Haven boardwalk, and then follows the coastline along Grand Haven State Park.

The scenery begins immediately at the corner of Washington and Fifth Streets with beautiful Central Park and its fountain and cool shade trees. Continue south on Fifth Street (which becomes Sheldon Road and then Lake Shore Drive), enjoying the breeze from Lake Michigan. Here the road is wide, with slow-moving traffic.

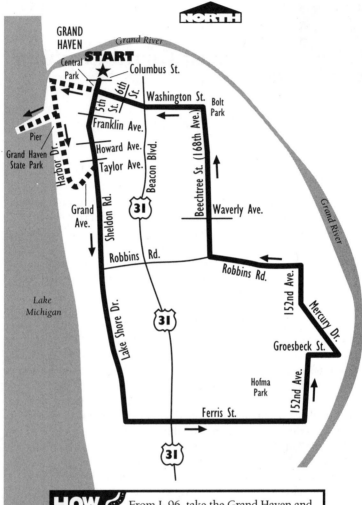

NORTH

GRAND HAVEN

Grand River

START

Central Park

Columbus St.

Washington St.

Bolt Park

6th St.

5th St.

Franklin Ave.

Howard Ave.

Taylor Ave.

Beechtree St. (168th Ave.)

Pier

Grand Haven State Park

Harbor Dr.

Beacon Blvd.

Waverly Ave.

Grand Ave.

Sheldon Rd.

31

Robbins Rd.

Robbins Rd.

152nd Ave.

Mercury Dr.

Lake Michigan

Lake Shore Dr.

31

Groesbeck St.

Hofma Park

152nd Ave.

Grand River

Ferris St.

31

31

HOW to get there From I–96, take the Grand Haven and Spring Lake exit. Drive west on M–104. Follow U.S. 31 (Beacon Boulevard) south and turn right onto Washington Street. Turn right onto Fifth Street and cross Columbus Street. The city parking lot is on the right.

DIREC-TIONS at a glance

0.0 From corner of Fifth and Columbus Streets, ride back south on Fifth Street (will change its name to Sheldon Road and then Lake Shore Drive), crossing Washington Street.

0.1 Cross Franklin Avenue after stop sign.

0.3 Continue straight after four-way stop at Howard Avenue.

0.8 Continue straight after four-way stop at Taylor Avenue.

1.0 Four-way stop at Grand Avenue. Beach route joins longer route here. Look for bike path on east side of Lake Shore Drive.

1.3 Continue straight after four-way stop at Robbins Road.

3.9 Turn left onto Ferris Street.

4.5 Cross railroad tracks.

4.6 Cross 168th Avenue and U.S. 31. *Caution:* Divided highway. Then veer right to follow Ferris Street.

6.6 Road dead-ends into 152nd Avenue. Turn left.

7.9 Stop and turn right onto Groesbeck Street.

8.3 Road dead-ends into Mercury Drive. Turn left to ride bike path or ride the road.

8.5 Stop and continue straight at Lake Avenue.

9.0 Leave the bike path, cross Mercury Drive, and turn right at 152nd Avenue.

9.7 Road curves and becomes Robbins Road.

10.4 Stop at Mercury Drive. Cross Robbins Road and then Mercury Drive to ride bike path or ride the road.

11.7 At traffic light turn right onto Beechtree (168th Avenue) and ride bike path north.

12.4 Stoplight at Waverly Avenue.

12.8 Turn left onto Washington Street.

13.3 Four-way stop at North Ferry Street.

13.5 Stoplight at Beacon Boulevard. *Caution:* Washington Street has a right-hand turn lane, so cars turn into your path. Also, the divider in the middle of Beacon Boulevard/U.S. 31 has no cut in curb for sidewalk. Walk bike across or move into center lane on Washington Street to ride with traffic.

13.6   Stoplight and then railroad tracks.

13.7   Cross Sixth Street. *Caution:* Curb has no cut.

13.8   Turn right onto Fifth Street.

13.9   Return to parking lot.

5.1 or 17.0 miles

0.0   From parking lot at Columbus and Fifth Streets, ride to Washington Street and turn right.

0.4   Turn left onto Harbor Drive, where Washington Street dead-ends.

1.0   Follow bike path to right at Y to ride to pier.

1.8   End of pier. *Caution:* Do not ride to end of pier if waves cover pier. Pier is slippery; check brakes. Watch also for wind, sand, and cracks. Turn around and ride pier back to asphalt bike path.

2.4   Turn right onto path to leave boardwalk area and enter Grand Haven State Park via South Harbor Drive.

2.5   Traffic light at park road.

3.3   Road curves left away from beach and becomes Grand Avenue. Ride road, as most curbs have no cuts.

4.1   Four-way stop at Sheldon Road. Turn right to join longer loop, or go left to ride 1.0 mile to parking lot.

By Grand Avenue, just as the road narrows, a bike path begins on the left. Trees replace houses as you move from residential to rural. After a left onto Ferris Street, you'll soon reach the intersection of U.S. 31 and Ferris Street, where there's a store with antiques and collectibles. Not much farther on Ferris Street, you'll think that you've time-traveled to Christmas because of the smell of a pine-tree farm, at 5.9 miles. Hofma Park is just 0.2 mile later—a good place for a break, with picnic tables, rest rooms, drinking water, nature trails, the Pottawattomie Bayou, and a unique floating bridge.

After 2 miles of trees and farmland comes a fantastic view, at 8.6 miles, of the Grand River. As you approach the bridge, you can see the river for miles, both to the east and west. Then the route begins to move back into the residential area. At 12.7 miles, Bolt Park has only a small piece of land at a corner, but it has big shade trees and benches. You may want to use it to enjoy some ice cream, which is available just 0.1 mile later, at the corner of Washington Street. Ride through more of Grand Haven's neighborhoods before crossing heavy traffic at Beacon Boulevard (U.S. 31). Then it's up a hill and back to Central Park and the starting point of the ride.

There's nothing like riding the Grand Haven pier out to the lighthouse; you'll get to do it on two of the loops. The only drawback of the pier extension is the challenging ride on Grand Avenue to Sheldon Road—the street is fairly narrow and very hilly, and the sidewalk is difficult to use because it has no cuts. *Use caution.*

For facing the challenge, however, you will be well rewarded. Riding west on Washington Street, you move into an area filled with great downtown shops. At the end of the street is the Tri-Cities Historical Museum in the old Grand Trunk Depot. Built in 1870, it was the terminus of Detroit, Grand Haven, and Milwaukee Railroad. Going south on Harbor Drive, you'll pick up the boardwalk, which leads to the pier and lighthouse. Test your brakes and *use caution,* as waves crashing over the sides of the pier leave puddles that can make the going slippery.

Leave the pier and ride south, following the beautiful beaches of Grand Haven State Park. Just before South Harbor Drive curves left into Grand Avenue, there is a restaurant right on the beach. After the challenging hills of Grand Avenue, you're back at Sheldon Road. Turn left for a short ride back to Central Park, or turn right to continue the longer ride. Either way, you'll enjoy a gentle Lake Michigan breeze.

Whitehall-Montague's Old Channel Trail

Number of miles:	16.4 (16.7 with loop to Weathervane Park)
Approximate pedaling time:	2 hours
Terrain:	Rolling hills, then flat
Traffic:	Light except in downtown Montague
Things to see:	World's largest weathervane, White Lake, Lake Michigan, Hart-Montague Bicycle Trail State Park
Food:	Ice-cream and convenience store at beginning; Indian Point Trading Post, 5.2 miles; Old Channel Inn, 5.9 miles; deli/convenience store, 14.7 miles

This ride has so many outstanding features that it's hard to mention them all: the largest weathervane in the world; a piece of the Hart-Montague Bicycle Trail State Park; great vistas of the shores of White Lake and Lake Michigan; historic White River Light Station Museum; and roads filled with rolling hills, curves, and tall trees that provide shade for the ride.

There are two ways to begin this scenic ride. The 16.7-mile loop follows the busy road of Business U.S. 31 to Weathervane Park, site of the famous weathervane, on the banks of White Lake. This hand-formed aluminum weathervane stands 48 feet tall and weighs 4,300 pounds. Whitehall-Montague is home to two of the largest manufacturers of weathervanes, so it's fitting to find the largest one ever made here. This loop passes Whitehall Products and Old Century Forge, both with their roofs adorned with every shape and size of weathervane.

The main loop (16.4 miles) eschews traffic, sticking to quieter

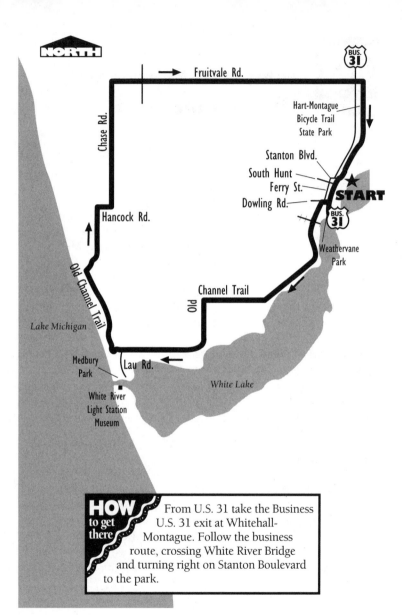

NORTH

Fruitvale Rd.

Chase Rd.

BUS. 31

Hart-Montague
Bicycle Trail
State Park

Stanton Blvd.

South Hunt

Ferry St.

Dowling Rd.

★ START

BUS. 31

Weathervane
Park

Hancock Rd.

Old Channel Trail

Channel Trail

Old

Lake Michigan

Medbury
Park

Lau Rd.

White River
Light Station
Museum

White Lake

HOW to get there

From U.S. 31 take the Business U.S. 31 exit at Whitehall-Montague. Follow the business route, crossing White River Bridge and turning right on Stanton Boulevard to the park.

DIREC-TIONS at a glance

0.0 Cross Business U.S. 31 to ride west on Stanton Boulevard. Stop at Bicycle Depot on corner to buy pass for Hart-Montague Trail. Halfway up the hill, turn left at Ferry Street.

0.3 Continue straight after stop sign at South Hunt.

0.4 Turn right onto Dowling Road and ride the sidewalk. (The 16.7-mile Weathervane Park route joins here.)

0.5 Halfway up the hill, turn left to cross road for Old Channel Trail. Trail marked with SHORELINE TRAIL signs; street signs say OLD CHANNEL TRAIL.

1.1 Railroad tracks at bottom of hill.

3.5 Stop and turn left, following Old Channel Trail. Street to right is Lamos Road. Wide bike shoulder begins here.

4.2 Wide shoulder lost on long downhill corner, but returns at top of next hill.

5.7 Road widens but wide shoulder lost.

8.4 Yield and turn right onto Hancock Road.

8.5 Turn left onto Chase Road.

10.5 Turn right onto Fruitvale Road, leaving SHORELINE TRAIL signs.

10.9 Go straight after stop sign.

14.7 Four-way stop at Business U.S. 31.

14.8 Turn right onto Hart-Montague Trail. Follow path.

16.4 Return to park.

16.7 miles

0.0 Cross Business U.S. 31 and buy pass for Hart-Montague Trail.

0.05 Ride south on Business U.S. 31. *Caution:* Traffic can be heavy.

0.5 Curve left, following Business U.S. 31.

0.6 Turn right into Ellenwood Dockominiums to Weathervane boardwalk and park.

0.65 Leaving Weathervane Park, turn left, heading north on Business U.S. 31

roads on the way to the Old Channel Trail. Both loops begin at the trail end of the Hart-Montague Bicycle Trail State Park. Built on a C&O Railroad right-of-way, the path starts in Hart and runs 22.5 miles south to Montague. The last part of this ride will include a small part of the Hart-Montague Trail. At trail end, or where the loops begin, there is a park with tables, rest rooms, and water.

From the park, cross Business U.S. 31 to buy a trail pass at the bicycle shop. The main loop continues past the shop, climbing the steepest hill on the ride. Halfway up the hill, turn left onto Ferry Street, which goes through a cute business area with old-fashioned streetlamps.

A right and a hill on Dowling Road bring you to the Old Channel Trail. Those who rode to Weathervane Park join the ride here. The ride is marked with SHORELINE TRAIL signs, as well as OLD CHANNEL TRAIL street signs. Roads are wide, and the speed limit is low. Also, motorists are used to bikers on these roads and watch out for them.

The Old Channel Trail follows the shore of White Lake, offering glimpses of it down below, through the trees on the left. Beautiful old houses with wrap-around porches and yards filled with large, majestic trees offer another lovely view on the right. Rolling hills and gentle curves also keep the ride interesting.

For a cold drink and snacks, try the Indian Point Trading Post, at 5.2 miles. The WHITE RIVER CHANNEL sign is just past it, at Lau Road. While the loop continues straight, turn left and ride a hilly mile-long road, veering right at the Y, for a rewarding view of the lighthouse at the White River Light Station Museum across the channel. Medbury Park is also here, offering a beautiful beach on Lake Michigan.

Back on the loop, at 5.9 miles, is the Old Channel Inn, a charming restaurant on Lake Michigan. After the inn and one more series of hills, the road flattens out. After passing the Old Channel Trail Golf Course, at 7.5 miles, the ride follows Chase Road, and you'll think you've been transported to Kansas without Toto because of the cornfields.

The Fruitvale Road stretch has several long hills and plenty of cornfields. It can get hot on this stretch of ride, so bring plenty of water. After crossing Business U.S. 31, turn right to join the Hart-Montague Trail. It's a short but peaceful stretch on the asphalt path back to the parking lot.

Lapping Lake Cadillac

Number of miles:	7.0
Approximate pedaling time:	1 hour
Terrain:	Mostly flat
Traffic:	Light
Things to see:	Lake Cadillac, Mitchell State Park, Kenwood Park Nature Area
Food:	Restaurants and stores on M–115, 2 blocks off route in downtown Cadillac, and stores before Kenwood Park Nature Area

Cadillac seems to be the gateway from western Michigan to the resort areas of northern Michigan. Many people never make it beyond Cadillac, however, and one of the reasons is the beauty of Mitchell State Park and beautiful Lake Cadillac. This short but scenic ride takes advantage of both.

Begin on the shores of Lake Mitchell at the state park day-use area. (Entering the park requires an annual or day pass.) Leaving the park, cross M–115 and pick up the bike path heading southeast. At the intersection of M–115 and M–55 you'll encounter a lot of traffic, but the bike path, which now follows M–55 along the lake, makes the going easy. The shore of Lake Cadillac almost immediately lies before you on the left.

Soon a curve to the left leads the path into a quiet residential area. The shore is so close that you can almost lean left on your bike and stick the toes of your foot in the water. When the road curves, the bike path becomes a wide shoulder on Sunnyside Drive. Ride next to the lake, or cross Sunnyside Drive to ride with the traffic. The views of Lake Cadillac are great on both sides.

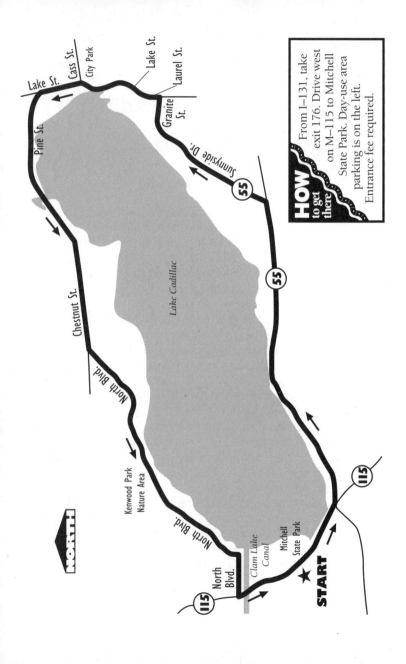

NORTH

Lake St. · Cass St. · City Park · Lake St. · Laurel St. · Granite St.

Pine St.

Chestnut St.

North Blvd.

Sunnyside Dr.

55

55

115

115

North Blvd.

Kenwood Park Nature Area

Lake Cadillac

Clam Lake Canal

Mitchell State Park

START

HOW to get there

From I-131, take exit 176. Drive west on M-115 to Mitchell State Park. Day-use area parking is on the left. Entrance fee required.

0.0 Leave parking lot and cross the street to ride on bike path. Turn right to ride path alongside east M–115. East M–55 crosses M–115 at stoplight. Ride through stoplight (bike path does not stop at light), following M–55.

0.6 East M–55 curves left (Sunnyside Drive), as does bike path. Bike path becomes wide shoulder. Ride alongside lake or cross street to ride shoulder with traffic.

2.9 Road curves right, and Sunnyside Drive becomes Granite Street. Bike path joins sidewalk

3.2 Turn left onto Laurel Street (east M–55 continues straight). Road curves and becomes Lake Street. Ride sidewalk on right side of road.

3.6 Bike path begins alongside road.

3.7 Stop and turn left to continue on Lake Street. (*Option:* Ride straight to visit downtown Cadillac.)

3.9 At stoplight turn left onto Pine Street. (Pine Street will turn into Chestnut Street.)

5.2 Veer left onto North Boulevard. Narrow shoulders.

6.1 Bike path through Kenwood Park Nature Area begins.

6.3 Bike path in nature area ends.

6.8 Clam Lake Canal on left.

6.9 Stop sign at M–115. Cross North Boulevard and ride bike path south on M–115 to state park entrance.

7.0 Cross road to reenter state park.

The road curves right to become Granite Street, and houses intrude between you and the lake. You'll make quick turns onto Laurel and Lake Streets, and then the route winds past City Park on the left. Lake Cadillac comes into view again. City Park has drinking water and rest rooms as well as a path along the shore. Unfortunately, no bike riding is allowed in the park; however, the vistas are just as beautiful from the bike path along the road. On the right is an old train depot.

While making a left onto Lake Street, you have the option of going straight to visit the downtown business area. Many unique shops make it a worthwhile trip and a change from the natural beauty of the lake.

After a left onto Pine Street, there is a path alongside the road. Veer left (oncoming traffic stops) onto North Boulevard, a quiet road lined with trees. The road and shoulder are narrow, but the road quickly widens, and soon you're at the Kenwood Park Nature Area, with rest rooms, drinking water, tables, and nature trails. Here you have the option to leave the bike lane and ride a bike path that enters the nature area and is closer to the shoreline.

Leaving the nature area, North Boulevard heads straight for the Clam Lake Canal, at 6.8 miles. The road curves and follows the canal toward Lake Mitchell. Dug in 1873, the canal connects the two lakes at the narrowest point. It was used to transport timber back when the lakes were called Big and Little Clam. One of the people who helped finance the canal was businessman George A. Mitchell. Now the one-third–mile-long canal is used by fishers, boaters, and many ducks.

From Lake Cadillac, the canal leads to M–115. Cross North Boulevard, the bridge over the canal, and ride the bike path on the east side of M–115. A short distance later, the ride ends at the state park day-use area on the right.

Three Cs and a Circle

Number of miles: 17.3
Approximate pedaling time: 2 hours
Terrain: Rolling hills
Traffic: Light
Things to see: North Higgins Lake State Park, Civilian Conservation Corps Museum, woods and wildflowers
Food: Concession stand at state park; pop machine at Super 8 Motel, 9.6 miles

This ride focuses on the Higgins Lake area. It offers a quiet ride on rolling hills, thousands of wildflowers along the roads, and hundreds of trees from pines to birches.

Officially, going by the distances listed for this ride, the route starts at North Higgins Lake State Park. Two other great spots are the Civilian Conservation Corps Museum, 0.2 mile east of the park entrance, and the Macmullan Conference Center at 0.4 mile east of the park entrance. The state park and CCC Museum require a daily or annual park pass. The conference center, when not being used, offers free parking.

A good reason to park at the CCC Museum is its fascinating look at a piece of Michigan history. It commemorates and celebrates all that the Civilian Conservation Corps did for the State of Michigan. People who spend time outdoors probably enjoy the fruits of the CCC's many labors every time they go to a state park or state forest.

When young men couldn't find jobs in the 1930s, President Franklin D. Roosevelt began the CCC to put them to work. More than 100,000 men in Michigan were given jobs in fish and game,

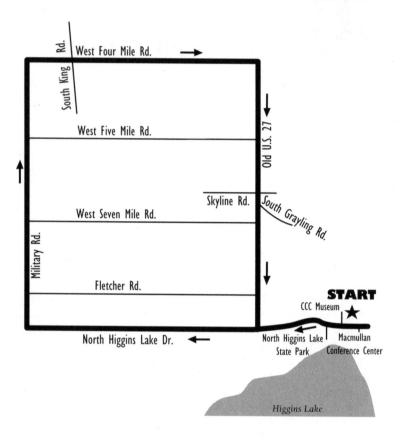

South King Rd.

West Four Mile Rd. →

West Five Mile Rd.

Old U.S. 27

Skyline Rd.

South Grayling Rd.

West Seven Mile Rd.

Military Rd.

Fletcher Rd.

START

CCC Museum ★

North Higgins Lake Dr. ←

North Higgins Lake State Park

Macmullan Conference Center

Higgins Lake

HOW to get there — From U.S. 27, take the Military Road exit. Go east on North Higgins Lake Drive, which leads to the North Higgins Lake State Park.

DIREC-TIONS at a glance

0.0 Ride left out of parking lot on North Higgins Lake Drive. Continue straight after blinking light and stop sign.
0.9 Turn right, north, onto Military Road.
2.6 Continue straight across Fletcher Road.
3.7 Continue straight across West Seven Mile Road.
5.7 Continue straight across West Five Mile Road.
6.7 Turn right onto West Four Mile Road.
7.6 Continue straight across South King Road.
9.7 Turn right onto Old U.S. 27.
10.9 Continue straight across West Five Mile Road.
11.7 Continue straight across Skyline Road.
12.1 Continue straight as South Grayling Road veers off to the left.
13.4 Continue straight across West Seven Mile Road.
14.7 Continue straight across Fletcher Road.
16.9 Turn left at blinking light onto North Higgins Lake Drive.
17.3 Turn right into state park entrance.

forestry, and state parks. They led the nation in the number of trees they planted—almost 500 million of them. They built campgrounds, made 7,000 miles of roads, and built hundreds of fire towers.

The museum compound has a path that leads you to different buildings and explains what the CCCers did in each, such as cone drying or seed collection. Walk to the museum building to see a map that shows where the camps were around the state. There's also an example of what the living conditions were like, showing sleeping cots, with CCCers' socks and pants hanging from lines above them.

The first stretch of the road, along North Higgins Lake Drive, is beautiful and quiet, as the rich tree cover on both sides of the road muffles noise from the campground and expressway. As you cross the expressway, the tree cover thins and the trees change from oaks and maples to pines on Military Road. There's no bike lane here, but the road is wide and traffic is light. Military Road develops curves and

rolling hills to keep things interesting. Wildflowers are everywhere; a particularly nice patch begins at 4.9 miles.

Beautiful old houses compete for your attention. A right turn onto West Four Mile Road brings a rise in the road and a nice stand of birches, at 6.7 miles. More wildflowers, in purple, blue, and pink, line the way in the seventh mile. The route continues to offer rolling hills and gentle curves. Flowers and trees are interrupted by a country club and a motel, at 8.8 and 9.6 miles respectively, just before crossing the expressway, at 9.7 miles.

After a right turn, the ride follows along the expressway for a short distance, then trees soon block those sights and sounds. After passing the Moose Lodge at the corner of South Grayling Road and Old U.S. 27, the ride straightens and flattens. This is the time to rest up for the hill that starts at 15.4 miles and continues until 16.2 miles. You're rewarded with a great downhill. This run leads to North Higgins Lake Drive and its deep-green canopy of trees. Turn left, and a short ride returns you to whichever point you chose to begin. (Don't miss the short but beautiful path along the beach in the campground.)

The Glen Lake Gallop

Number of miles:	18.2 (10.9 for shorter loop)
Approximate pedaling time:	3 hours
Terrain:	Rolling hills, several steep
Traffic:	Heavy during peak vacation weekends
Things to see:	Sleeping Bear Dunes National Lakeshore, Glen Lake, Dune Climb, town of Glen Arbor
Food:	Restaurants and stores in Glen Arbor; restaurant, 9.9 miles; store, 12.1 miles; restaurant, 12.4 miles; ice cream, 15.9 miles

Chippewa legend explains the massive sand dune on the northeast shore of Lake Michigan. A tremendous forest fire on the west coast of Lake Michigan drove a mother bear and her two cubs into the water, where they swam and swam. The mother reached the eastern shore and lay on a bluff, exhausted, waiting for her cubs. They couldn't reach the shore and drowned, forming the Manitou Islands. Where the mother lay waiting, now only a sand dune remains. And here the ride begins: the Sleeping Bear Dunes National Lakeshore.

This ride offers sweeping vistas of Lake Michigan and Glen Lake, hills and curves, birches and pines, and a dune climb. It starts by riding the shoulder of Pierce Stocking Scenic Drive to M–109.

Turn left onto M–109's wide shoulder, and soon Glen Lake is on the right, trees on the left. Curve right, and a long, fast downhill begins, with a great view to your right. At 0.6 mile, curve left; you'll see dunes in the distance as the road continues to curve. At 1.3 miles, you'll cruise downhill through a great arch formed by tree branches above the road. Eventually, tall dunes appear on the left, with Glen Lake on the right.

Pass a picnic area at 2.1 miles. The famous Dune Climb begins at 2.4 miles. Struggle up the steep wall of sand, or take a break and use the drinking water and rest rooms. At 2.7 miles, another picnic area is on the right. Begin a long steady uphill climb at 3.0 miles, and be rewarded with a great view of Lake Michigan at the top.

At 3.7 miles, turn right to stay on M–109; the wide shoulder continues. The road still has curves, but it flattens out. At 4.3 miles, pass the D. H. Day Campground, with beach access to Sleeping Bear Bay on Lake Michigan. Then enter Glen Arbor, with its cute shops, stores, and restaurants. Stop and continue straight, as M–109 ends at 5.8 miles, riding the shoulder of M–22 east, through Glen Arbor. (Shorter loop turns right here.)

At 6.6 miles, turn right onto CO 675 (Crystal View Road), where you'll immediately cross the Crystal River. Ride the shoulder, and at 7.0 miles, the river glistens through the trees on the left as the road becomes South Dunn's Farm Road. The flat is broken, at 8.4 miles, with a long, hard hill. Here again the work pays off, with a wonderful scene of Glen Lake. Use the view as your excuse to stop and catch your breath. Pedal past a restaurant at 9.9 miles, and the trees fall behind to allow a view of the lake.

Pass the Old Settlers Picnic Grounds, at 11.9 miles, as you move into Burdickville. Just before a store, CO 616 joins CO 675. More of the lake is visible at 12.4 miles, as you pass the Glen Lake Inn. After a series of sharp curves, CO 675 turns left as you continue straight on the rolling hills of CO 616. At 13.5 miles begin the longest and hardest uphill. You'll be thrilled when you reach 14.0—the top of the hill. A great place to celebrate is Inspiration Point, just at the beginning of the downhill run. It affords a beautiful treetop view of Glen Lake. Continue the run downhill through a cool, dark canopy of trees. *Use caution*, as some of the downhills are steep. Once again Glen Lake is visible at 15.4 miles.

Stop and turn left onto M–22, at 15.9 miles. Ride it until 16.7 miles, and turn right on West Welch Road. This wide road curves immediately left, and rolling hills begin. Get ready for one more steep

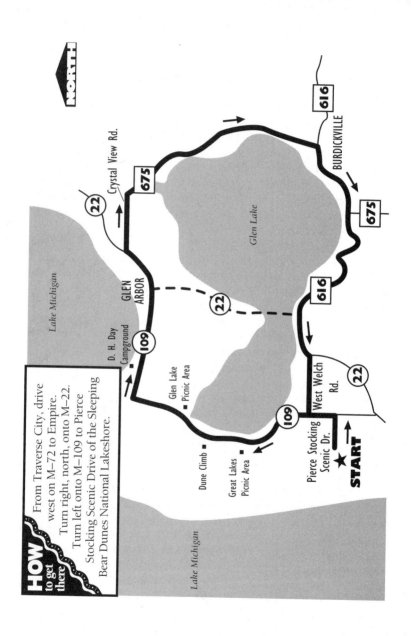

NORTH

HOW to get there

From Traverse City, drive west on M-72 to Empire. Turn right, north, onto M-22. Turn left onto M-109 to Pierce Stocking Scenic Drive of the Sleeping Bear Dunes National Lakeshore.

Lake Michigan

Glen Lake

Lake Michigan

Crystal View Rd.

22

675

616

BURDICKVILLE

675

616

22

GLEN ARBOR

109

D. H. Day Campground

Glen Lake
■ Picnic Area

West Welch Rd.

109

Pierce Stocking Scenic Dr.

★ START

Dune Climb ■

Great Lakes
■ Picnic Area

0.0 Turn left out of parking lot to return to entrance of Pierce Stocking Scenic Drive.

0.2 Turn left onto M–109.

2.1 Pass Great Lakes Picnic area on left.

2.4 Pass Dune Climb on left.

2.7 Glen Lake Picnic Area on right.

3.7 Turn right to remain on M–109.

4.3 Pass D. H. Day Campground on left.

5.8 Stop and continue straight on M–22. M–109 ends.

6.6 Turn right onto CO 675 (Crystal View Road).

11.9 Pass Old Settlers Picnic Grounds on right.

12.1 CO 616 joins CO 675.

13.4 Continue straight on CO 616, as CO 675 turns left.

15.9 Stop and turn left onto M–22.

16.7 Turn right onto West Welch Road.

17.8 Stop and turn left onto M–109.

18.0 Turn right onto Pierce Stocking Scenic Drive.

18.2 Turn right into parking lot of Sleeping Bear Dunes National Lakeshore.

10.9 miles

0.0 Turn left out of parking lot to return to entrance of Pierce Stocking Scenic Drive.

0.2 Turn left onto M–109.

3.7 Turn right to remain on M–109.

5.8 Stop and turn right onto M–22, leaving longer loop.

8.6 Curve right at intersection of M–22 and CO 616. Rejoin longer loop here.

9.4 Turn right onto West Welch Road.

10.5 Stop and turn left onto M–109.

10.7 Turn right onto Pierce Stocking Scenic Drive.

10.9 Turn right into parking lot of Sleeping Bear Dunes National Lakeshore.

uphill that leads to the stop sign at 17.8 miles. Turn left to ride back on M–109. At 18.0 miles, return to Pierce Stocking Scenic Drive, where a right turn leads to the parking lot, finishing this spectacular ride of deep water, high dunes, and tall trees at 18.2 miles.

The shorter loop won't get you out of the hills completely, but it does have fewer hills and avoids the largest ones. Follow the longer loop up until 5.8 miles, the intersection of M–22 and M–109. Turn right and ride M–22 as it slices through Glen Lake. This 2.8-mile stretch is beautiful: rolling hills, sparkling water, tall trees, intersecting curves, and all of them enjoyed while riding a nice shoulder. At 8.6 miles the route joins the longer loop and follows it home.

The Leland Loop

Number of miles:	14.4
Approximate pedaling time:	2 hours
Terrain:	Small rolling hills
Traffic:	Possibly heavy during summer weekends
Things to see:	Lake Leelanau and picturesque town of Leland
Food:	Leland and town of Lake Leelanau

Fishtown may not sound romantic or the place to be, but that's what keeps bringing tourists to Leland. Perched on the banks of the Carp River, between Lakes Michigan and Leelanau, weather-beaten gray shanties used to hold fishing gear. Now most of these turn-of-the-century buildings house businesses, and fishnets hang out here along with the tourists from Chicago and Detroit.

You'll pass the Historic District of Fishtown, where you can purchase delicious smoked whitefish or charter a boat, on the way to Pearl Street, at the end of the ride. This trip also features a shore-hugging loop around the northern section of Lake Leelanau, passing through the town of Lake Leelanau and offering easy pedaling on mostly flat roads.

To begin, park on Pearl Street or anywhere else you're able to during busy summer weekends. From Main Street and Pearl, turn right, heading north on M–22, and ride on paved shoulders. Curve right, and you're out of town, riding a nice, wide shoulder up a small hill, with trees lining the road.

Curves continue, as well as the uphill, as you pass a cemetery, at 1.4 miles. Here the road is called Manitou Trail. Soon the lake may be

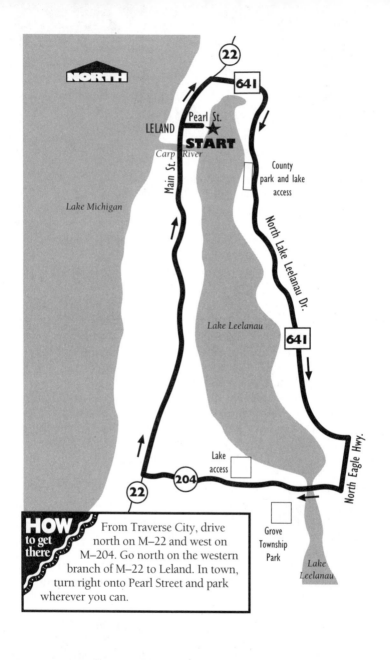

NORTH

22

641

Pearl St.
LELAND
★
START
Carp River

County park and lake access

Lake Michigan

Main St.

North Lake Leelanau Dr.

Lake Leelanau

641

641

North Eagle Hwy.

Lake access

22

204

Grove Township Park

Lake Leelanau

HOW to get there — From Traverse City, drive north on M–22 and west on M–204. Go north on the western branch of M–22 to Leland. In town, turn right onto Pearl Street and park wherever you can.

0.0 From Pearl Street and Main Street, turn right and ride north on M–22.

3.1 Turn right onto CO 641 (North Lake Leelanau Drive).

3.8 County park and lake access.

8.4 Stop and turn right onto North Eagle Highway.

8.8 Stop, turn right onto M–204, and ride into the village of Lake Leelanau.

9.0 Ride bridge over Lake Leelanau.

9.5 Grove Township Park.

10.3 Lake access.

12.2 Stop and turn right onto M–22.

13.4 Enter village of Leland.

14.3 Ride bridge over Carp River.

14.4 Turn right onto Pearl Street and return to parking area.

seen between the trees. At 3.1 miles, turn right onto CO 641—a little-traveled road with no shoulder. Trees hide the lake at first, then a curve left brings the road to the water's edge. Here the road winds, with the shore on the right and pine trees on the left.

Pass a beach area with picnic tables, at 3.8 miles, before the trees block the view. After riding up a small hill, you'll reach an open section passing close to a steep drop to the lake. First apple trees, then birches and pines decorate the roadside as the route enters another section of curves. At 7.0 miles, ride a long uphill and curve left for a view high above the lake. At 7.8 miles, enjoy a long downhill.

Curve left and right before the stop sign at 8.4 miles. Turn right, onto North Eagle Highway. Then stop again at 8.8 miles, turning right, onto M–204, into the town of Lake Leelanau. The bridge at 9.0 miles crosses the lake at one of its narrowest points. Lake Leelanau offers plenty of places to buy picnic supplies and snacks.

A long ride uphill takes you out of town on a wide, paved shoulder. M–204 winds away from the lake, with curves and uphills, on its way to the intersection with M–22. Stop and turn right onto M–22, at 12.2 miles. Here again is a wide paved shoulder.

More curves bring the road close to the lake. With great vistas and easy riding, you'll be at the WELCOME TO LELAND sign before you know it. Trees move in, only to move out again, revealing Lake Leelanau. Houses and businesses begin, and at 14.3 miles, the route crosses the Carp River, with Fishtown on the left. *Carefully* weave your way through distracted walkers and drivers on the way to the right turn onto Pearl Street, at 14.4 miles, and the conclusion of the ride.

The Old Mission Amble

Number of miles:	31.4 (6.9 for shorter loop)
Approximate pedaling time:	4 hours
Terrain:	Hills, one very steep
Traffic:	Moderate
Things to see:	Old Mission Point State Park with lighthouse, sweeping vistas of Grand Traverse Bay, Old Mission
Food:	Country stores, 9.8 and 27.7 miles

Although it has spectacular Grand Traverse Bay vistas in any season, this becomes a not-to-be-missed ride during May, when thousands of cherry trees are adorned with blossoms. This route features rolling hills through some of the area where one third of the world's cherries are grown.

The narrow Old Mission Peninsula divides Grand Traverse Bay, the second-largest bay on Lake Michigan, into an East Arm and West Arm. Both are featured on this ride, along with birches and pines, one of Michigan's oldest lighthouses, and the Old Mission.

Interestingly, this ride begins on the forty-fifth parallel, which is exactly midway between the equator and the North Pole, at the tip of Mission Peninsula. At this location, Old Mission Point State Park has a sandy beach for sunbathing, pit toilets, and a lighthouse built in 1870. Head south out of the park on M–37 (Center Road), riding the curves, with the water visible through the trees on the right. At 0.8 mile, the view opens, offering a view of a wide sweep of Grand Traverse Bay, with all shades of blue.

Hills begin at 2.4 miles, and you're soon rolling past vineyards. As you begin going downhill, turn right onto Old Mission Road, at 3.4

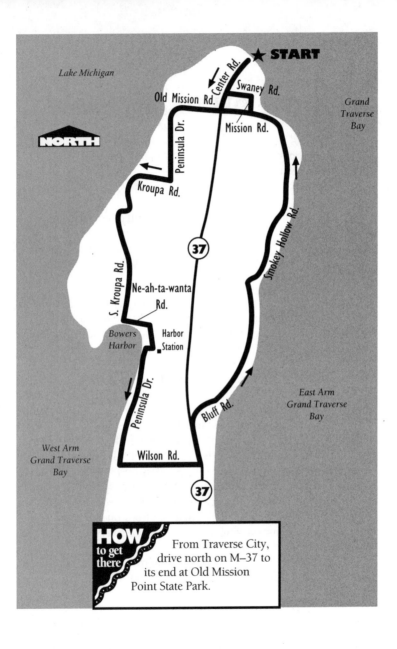

★ START

Lake Michigan

Grand Traverse Bay

NORTH

Center Rd.

Swaney Rd.

Old Mission Rd.

Mission Rd.

Peninsula Dr.

Kroupa Rd.

37

S. Kroupa Rd.

Ne-ah-ta-wanta Rd.

Smokey Hollow Rd.

Bowers Harbor

Harbor Station

Peninsula Dr.

Bluff Rd.

East Arm Grand Traverse Bay

West Arm Grand Traverse Bay

Wilson Rd.

37

HOW to get there

From Traverse City, drive north on M–37 to its end at Old Mission Point State Park.

DIRECTIONS at a glance

0.0	Leave Old Mission Point State Park via M–37 South.
3.4	Turn right onto Old Mission Road.
3.9	Road curves left and becomes Peninsula Drive.
5.9	Turn right onto Kroupa Road. Becomes South Kroupa Road.
8.4	Stop and turn left onto Ne-ah-ta-wanta Road.
9.6	Stop and turn right onto Peninsula Drive at the Harbor Station toward Bowers Harbor.
15.5	Turn left onto Wilson Road.
16.3	Stop and turn left onto M–37.
18.1	Turn right onto Bluff Road.
24.7	Stop and turn right onto Smokey Hollow Road.
27.5	Turn right onto Mission Road.
28.5	Stop and turn left onto Swaney Road.
30.0	Stop and turn right onto Center Road.
31.4	Return to park.

6.9 miles

0.0	Leave Old Mission Point State Park via Center Road, M–37.
3.4	Turn left onto Old Mission Road.
3.9	Turn left to follow Mission Road.
4.7	Stop and turn left onto Swaney Road.
5.5	Stop and turn right onto Center Road.
6.9	Return to state park.

miles. No shoulder but the road has low traffic volume. The shorter ride turns left here. Pass cherries on the left and grapes on the right before curving into Peninsula Drive. A flat respite is broken at 4.3 miles with a long uphill. But there's a rewarding view at the top.

Continue winding through curves and hills on Kroupa Road. After a sharp left curve, at 6.7 miles, the road flattens. More curves and hills lead to a left turn on Ne-ah-ta-wanta Road. Turn right, at 9.6 miles, into Bowers Harbor, where there's a country store. Curve left here; this section offers some of the best views of Grand Traverse Bay, with plenty of curves and lake views, and a nice shoulder to enjoy them on.

Turn left onto Wilson Road, at 15.5 miles, and climb a steep hill that has a panoramic view at the top. Ride downhill, then turn left onto M–37 and ride the wide shoulder, with the East Arm of the bay close by. At 18.1 miles, turn right onto Bluff Road, where traffic moves slowly on the wide road. Curve left, and the beach lies before you. From 18.2 to 18.6 miles, ride a long uphill. Then at 18.9 miles enjoy a spectacular view of trees and water.

Bluff and then Smokey Hollow Roads are characterized by hills, curves, and watery vistas or tall tree canopies. A right turn at 27.5 miles leads to the Old Mission Market, with snacks and drinks, and then the replica of the Old Mission Church. Originally built in 1839 by the Reverend Peter Dougherty, the replica has the bell from the original church. It also offers displays on the history of the mission and the area.

Continue riding through the trees to Swaney Road. Turn left, and ride the winding road to M–37 (Center Road). Turn right; now you can enjoy more views of Grand Traverse Bay while returning to the park, at 31.4 miles.

The Lake Charlevoix Loop

Number of miles:	34.0
Approximate pedaling time:	4 hours
Terrain:	Gently rolling hills
Traffic:	Heavy on weekends on M–66 and U.S. 31
Things to see:	Historic Horton Bay General Store, Ironton Chain Ferry, Charlevoix, Boyne City
Food:	All along route

Tourists have flocked to Charlevoix since the 1800s, and for good reason. Everything seems to sparkle on a sunny day. Maybe that's because the town is wedged between Lakes Michigan, Round, and Charlevoix. Or maybe it's the glittering merchandise in the quaint tourist shops. Whatever the reason, it's the perfect start for a scenic ride.

Ride west, leaving the Charlevoix High School parking lot, and turn right along pansy-lined U.S. 31. A steep downhill leads to shops and views of Round Lake. Then cross the drawbridge, where tall-masted sailboats make their way to Lake Michigan.

Climb uphill, riding the sidewalk or road. Traffic can be heavy during the summer, so *use caution* until 1.7 miles, when the road narrows to two lanes and has a nice wide shoulder. At 2.5 miles, turn right onto C 56 (Boyne City Road). Wide lanes make this a comfortable road to ride; the curves and rolling hills make it enjoyable.

On C 56, Lake Charlevoix keeps popping through the tall trees. At 7.9 miles, pass a thick stand of pines before reaching a panoramic view of the lake. Slow down at 9.4 miles for a cemetery on the left

and an old schoolhouse on the right. The roadside attractions continue at 10.3 miles, with a herd of llamas on the left.

Ride the curves into Horton Bay—and Hemingway country. Ernest Hemingway spent part of his youth at his parents' home on Walloon Lake, northeast of Lake Charlevoix. The writer married his first wife in a local church in 1921; a copy of his marriage license hangs on the wall of the Horton Bay General Store, at 11.8 miles. The store was mentioned in Hemingway's story *Up in Michigan.* As you leave Horton Bay, don't miss the treehouse on the right, which has a "royal box" where the "high society" of Horton Bay meet.

At 15.5 miles, a wide shoulder announces Young State Park within 0.4 mile. Turn right to visit and ride the bike lane to the beach. The park has drinking water, rest rooms, and plenty of beautiful picnic areas on the Lake Charlevoix shore.

Back on the route, enter Boyne City limits, at 16.3 miles, and continue riding the shoulder. Lakeside parks begin at 18.0 miles, with pavilions and rest rooms. As you leave the city, the road has a wide shoulder, which branches off as a bike path, at 18.8 miles. The path hugs the shoreline, offering some of the most spectacular views of the lake.

Less than a mile later, move back onto the road to ride into the town of Advance, at 21.2 miles. Pass a country store and you're on Ferry Road. Tall trees shade the road for most of the ride over rolling hills. For a break, there's Whiting County Park, at 23.2 miles.

Ride a great downhill to 28.2 miles and board the famous Ironton Chain Ferry—with its cable guiding the barge across the lake. The south arm of Lake Charlevoix is on the left. Operating since the 1870s, the ferry carries only a few cars, but it always has room for another bicycle, for a nominal fee.

When you land, ride a steep hill and veer to the right on Ferry Road. Stop and turn right onto M–66's nice shoulder. The hills flatten out after 30 miles, on your way back to Charlevoix. At 33.1 miles, a bike route begins on a wide sidewalk and turns right alongside U.S. 31. Fast-food restaurants replace the trees and wildflowers along this section of the route as the ride returns to Charlevoix High School, at 34.0 miles.

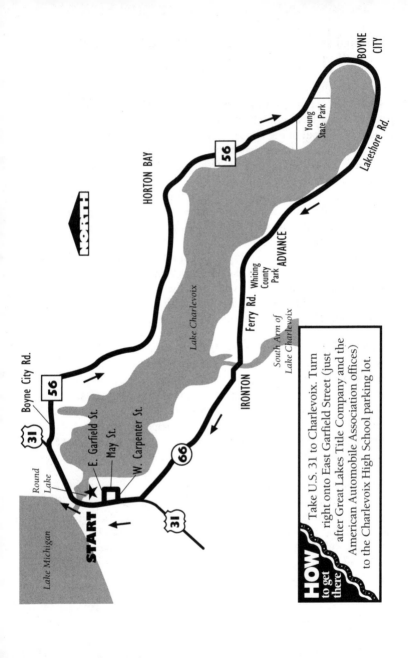

NORTH

Lake Michigan

Round Lake

31
Boyne City Rd.
56

START

E. Garfield St.
May St.
W. Carpenter St.

31

66

IRONTON

South Arm of Lake Charlevoix

Lake Charlevoix

HORTON BAY

56

Young State Park

BOYNE CITY

Lakeshore Rd.

ADVANCE

Whiting County Park

Ferry Rd.

HOW to get there

Take U.S. 31 to Charlevoix. Turn right onto East Garfield Street (just after Great Lakes Title Company and the American Automobile Association offices) to the Charlevoix High School parking lot.

0.0   Turn left out of the Charlevoix High School parking lot and head west on East Garfield Street.

0.2   Turn right onto U.S. 31 to ride into downtown Charlevoix.

2.5   Turn right onto C 56 (Boyne City Road).

4.1   Historic Greensky Hill Indian Methodist Church turnoff.

16.3   Enter Boyne City; road becomes West Michigan Street.

17.2   Road curves right and becomes North Lake Street.

18.2   Traffic light.

18.3   Turn right onto Main Street at four-way stop.

18.4   Road curves left and becomes Front Street, and eventually Lakeshore Road.

21.5   Enter village of Advance.

21.6   Pass FERRY OPEN sign; road becomes Ferry Road.

28.2   Ride Ironton Chain Ferry across small section of Lake Charlevoix. After ferry ride, continue on Ferry Road. Road curves right.

28.4   Stop and turn right onto M–66.

33.3   At traffic light, turn right onto U.S. 31.

33.6   Turn right onto West Carpenter Street.

33.8   Stop and turn left onto May Street.

34.0   Turn left into Charlevoix High School parking lot.

The Tunnel of Trees

Number of miles: 18.4
Approximate pedaling time: 3 hours
Terrain: Rolling hills
Traffic: Light
Things to see: Tunnels formed by tall trees, vistas of Lake Michigan through hardwoods, Cross Village, Good Hart, historic Legs Inn
Food: In Cross Village and Good Hart

It's the sweetheart of cyclists, and for good reason: a narrow, winding road shunned by most motorists, lined with tall hardwoods whose branches rise and arch to form an expansive canopy shading smooth asphalt. The deep greens of ferns and trees are interrupted only by the clear blues of Lake Michigan. It's M–119, running from Cross Village to Harbor Springs. This ride features the especially scenic section from Cross Village to Good Hart.

Begin in Cross Village, home of historic Legs Inn, created by Polish immigrant Stanley Smolak. You can't miss the legs that stick straight up in the air and decorate the lower roofline, or the tepee by the parking lot, constructed of huge sections of bark. The restaurant, built with fieldstone and wood, offers a stone fireplace, a Polish and American menu, and hand-carved furniture made from all types of wood pieces, from tree stumps to roots. During the summer, service extends to the bluff overlooking Lake Michigan behind the restaurant.

Park in front of the inn, or the convenience store. Then ride south on twisting M–119—a road on which they don't even bother to paint a center line. Soon trees edge the road and the curves begin. At 0.9

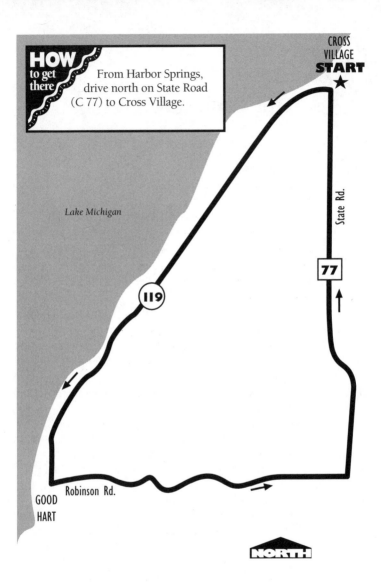

HOW to get there From Harbor Springs, drive north on State Road (C 77) to Cross Village.

CROSS VILLAGE
START ★

Lake Michigan

State Rd.

77

119

Robinson Rd.

GOOD HART

NORTH

DIREC- TIONS at a glance

0.0	Leave Cross Village, riding south on M–119.
7.0	Enter Good Hart.
7.3	Turn left onto Robinson Road.
12.1	Stop and turn left onto State Road (C 77).
18.3	Stop and turn right, north, into Cross Village.
18.4	Enter Cross Village.

mile, curve left and up to view Lake Michigan through the trees. More small ups and downs lead to a superb lake overlook at 2.6 miles. Then move into a fairly flat stretch, with the lake behind the trees.

The curves continue to the spectacular panoramic view of the lake at 5.7 miles. Enter Good Hart, at 7.0 miles, and pass the general store on the right. If your legs are warmed up enough, get ready for some bigger hills. If you're not ready for big hills, or just really enjoyed the famous Tunnel of Trees, turn around and ride back the picturesque way you came. To try something different, turn left onto Robinson Road and immediately ride a short, steep uphill, lined with pines. At the top, take a breather and look behind you for a great lake view. At 8.1 miles, begin pedaling a series of hills and curves.

Trees soon give way to fields and farms, but the trees return at the downhill and left curve, at 9.9 miles. Another long downhill at 11.4 miles turns and twists before reaching the stop sign at 12.1 miles.

Turn left onto State Road (C 77). This road, like Robinson Road, offers hills and curves past trees and fields. Enjoy a great view of the area as you ride a straight downhill at 12.5 miles.

About 17.4 miles, pass stately old barns and houses before cruising past the CROSS VILLAGE sign, at 18.0 miles. As you enter the village there is a large convenience store on the right. Curve left and then stop, at 18.3 miles. Turn right, and look skyward to follow the Legs Inn's wooden legs to the starting point, at 18.4 miles.

Circling Mackinac Island

Number of miles:	8.1
Approximate pedaling time:	1 hour
Terrain:	Mostly flat
Traffic:	Heavy bike, horse, and pedestrian traffic on holiday weekends
Things to see:	Mackinac Bridge, Fort Mackinac, Arch Rock, British Landing Nature Center
Food:	All along southeast side of island; snacks at intersection of Lakeshore and British Landing Roads, 4.6 miles

With automobiles prohibited, Mackinac Island, in the Straits of Mackinac, is a bicyclist's dream. Bikers ride alongside horse-drawn carriages and hikers, on miles and miles of paved roads and paths that circle and crisscross the 3-mile-long island.

The island's name comes from a shortened version of the Indian word *Michilimackinac*, or "large turtle," a reference to the shape of the island. This ride, filled with military history and incredible vistas, features 8.1 miles of mostly flat land, along both woods and coastline, while traveling the island's perimeter.

With your bike, ride a ferry from either St. Ignace or Mackinaw City. After landing on Mackinac Island, turn right and bike Main Street to the Visitors Center, where the ride begins. Here is the heart of the island's activity, with fudge and souvenir shops and quaint boutiques.

Ride east from the Visitors Center on Huron Street, and almost immediately pass Fort Mackinac, high atop a hill on the left. Fort Mackinac today operates as it did in the 1800s, with soldiers parading

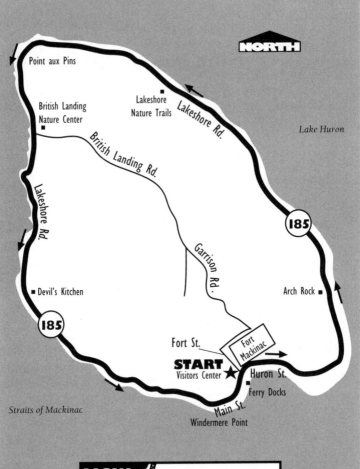

NORTH

Point aux Pins

British Landing
Nature Center

Lakeshore
Nature Trails

Lakeshore Rd.

Lake Huron

British Landing Rd.

Lakeshore Rd.

185

Garrison Rd.

Devil's Kitchen

Arch Rock

185

Fort St.

Fort
Mackinac

START
Visitors Center

Huron St.
Ferry Docks

Straits of Mackinac

Main St.

Windermere Point

HOW
to get
there
There is ferry service to
Mackinac Island from both
Mackinaw City and St. Ignace.

DIREC-TIONS at a glance

0.0 From the ferry docks, ride east to the Visitors Center, on the left side of the street. Ride begins here on Main Street, which soon changes to Huron Street.

0.1 Island House on left.

0.3 St. Anne Church.

0.4 Mission Church.

1.0 Arch Rock and Spring Trail.

2.8 Lakeshore Nature Trails.

4.6 Continue straight past British Landing Road.

6.8 Devil's Kitchen.

7.4 Boardwalk begins.

7.9 Windermere Point.

8.1 Visitors Center.

on drill and shooting muskets and cannons. The British built the fort in the 1700s, taking advantage of the island's high bluffs and deep harbor to protect its million-dollar fur trade.

Take a break and visit the fort, or continue on Huron Street around the island's perimeter. Soon you'll hear the lake lapping against the shore. Nestled between Lake Huron and high cliffs and rock formations, the road curves and becomes Lakeshore Road. Strangely enough for a road without automobile traffic, the road is also considered a state route, designated M–185.

At 1.0 mile, pass Arch Rock, which is shaped like a bridge. Wooden steps lead to the top. Legend tells of an Indian girl who fell in love with the sky spirit's son. When the girl's father denied them marriage, she cried until her tears eroded the middle of the rock, and only an arch remained.

Continue on the winding road, past the Lakeshore Nature Trails, a 300-yard-long wildflower trail. Halfway around the perimeter, you reach Point aux Pins, or Point of Pines. Through the trees on the western side of the island you can glimpse Mackinac Bridge, a very long suspension bridge. Even though the towers of the Golden Gate and Verrazano Narrows Bridges are higher and farther apart, this 5-mile-long bridge, weighing in at more than one million tons, is longer.

At 4.6 miles, find the British Landing Nature Center, with picnic tables and rest rooms. Just past this is British Landing Road, which bisects the island. This is where the British landed during the War of 1812 and then marched to Fort Mackinac to battle the Americans—another good road to ride. A store on the corner offers snacks and cold drinks.

Continue straight, enjoying a wonderful stretch of road along the beach, at 5.4 miles. And 0.6 mile later you can watch the rooster tails of the ferries as they zip across the water to St. Ignace.

The Devil's Kitchen, at 6.8 miles, offers a look at a group of small sea caves. Soon you're passing the boardwalk, at 7.4 miles, and then houses begin to sprout on the left. A final curve to the left and you're back winding your way between carriages, past shops, to the Visitors Center at 8.1 miles.

The De Tour Tour

Number of miles: 22.6
Approximate pedaling time: 3 hours
Terrain: Rolling hills
Traffic: Light
Things to see: Sweeping vistas of Lake Huron, St. Mary's River, De Tour Village, Caribou Lake
Food: De Tour Village; country store, 19.6 miles

Leave the tourist madness of the Straits of Mackinac behind for the quiet beauty of Lake Huron and De Tour Village. M–134 forms the backbone for this ride; this is considered one of the most scenic roads in the state. The lake is only a few footsteps away along most of this winding road, and the sweeping views of coves are breathtaking.

Begin in De Tour Village, known as the jumping-off point for Drummond Island. The village offers several fine restaurants, the De Tour Passage Historical Museum, and views of where the St. Mary's River joins Lake Huron. Located at the Strait of De Tour Passage, De Tour was named by French explorers as the "turning point" to Mackinac Island and was used as a stop on the way there.

Start at the De Tour Area School; ride east and then turn north onto M–134. M–134 soon turns right, where it runs to the ferry dock for boats to Drummond Island. (This also is where you'll find the historical museum—a great place to explore before or after the ride.) The route, however, continues straight, where the road becomes Ontario Street, soon leaving De Tour Village behind. Make a sharp left onto Democrat Road. This road's wide lanes run up and down small

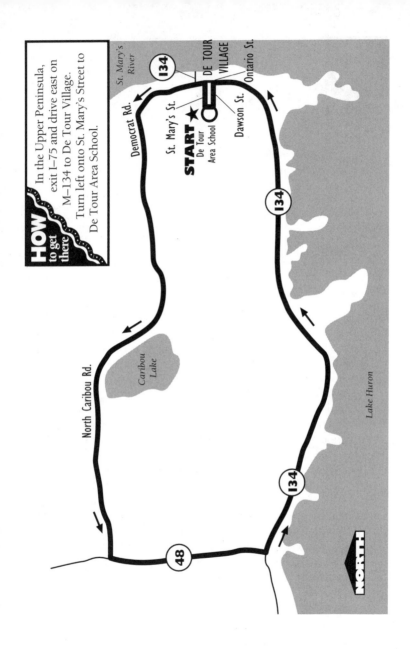

DIREC-TIONS at a glance

0.0	Leave De Tour Area School parking lot by turning left onto Dawson Street.
0.2	Stop and turn left onto Ontario Street (M–134).
0.3	Continue straight on Ontario Street as M–134 turns right.
0.8	Sharp left onto Democrat Road. Road becomes North Caribou Road.
4.9	Pass Caribou Lake on left.
9.5	Stop and turn left onto M–48.
12.6	Stop and turn left onto M–134.
15.1	Roadside park.
19.6	Country store.
20.8	De Tour Village limits.
22.4	Turn left at blinking light onto St. Mary's Street.
22.6	Return to De Tour Area School parking lot.

hills lined with wildflowers and several types of evergreen trees.

Democrat Road becomes North Caribou Road, and Caribou Lake shows itself between the trees on the left by 4.9 miles. Curves join the hills at the public lake access, at 5.8 miles. A straight and flat stretch, at 6.9 miles, introduces a swampy area filled with cattails. More small hills or humps lead to M–48, at 9.5 miles. Turn left and ride this low-traffic road with towering pines on both sides. The road has curves and hills, also.

M–48 ends at M–134, where the route turns left. You only have to ride 0.2 mile on the shoulder before seeing a nice view of Lake Huron, where colorful birches and pines frame the water. Curve left, and at 13.6 miles, the road opens up with dunes on the right. That's a great spot to pull off and get sand in your shoes.

At 15.1 miles, a roadside park filled with pines has picnic tables, drinking water, and toilets. The coastline becomes rocky as you pass a state campground, at 16.5 miles. M–134 continues to curve left and right as it follows the coves of the coastline. It's finally broken by a

straight stretch, at 18.6 miles. A country store follows a mile later. The next 2 miles are filled with more breathtaking vistas.

A marshy area with wildflowers and cattails on the right heralds the De Tour Village limits. Curve left; the marsh continues. Grab another look at a Lake Huron cove at the pull-off at 21.6 miles. At 22.1 miles, pass the Shula F. Giddens Memorial Gardens, a restful place with flowers and benches in memory of a teacher and community leader. Then an uphill run takes the route to the blinking light at St. Mary's Street. Turn left and return to De Tour Area School, at 22.6 miles, leaving the lake behind.

The Big Spring:
Kitch-iti-Kipi

Number of miles:	15.5
Approximate pedaling time:	2 hours
Terrain:	Gently rolling hills
Traffic:	Light
Things to see:	Indian Lake State Park, Palms Book State Park, raft ride over Michigan's largest spring, birches and pines
Food:	Snacks at Palms Book State Park, 6.6 miles, and Linda's Breadbox, 11.4 miles

Legend has it that a young warrior was trying to win the hand of a fair but fickle maiden. She would submit to his wooing only if he could catch her in his canoe as she jumped from a bough. The brave Kitch-iti-kipi drowned in the spring in the attempt, however, and that's why it is named after him. Another version—more bland—says that *Kitch-iti-kipi* is the Ojibway word for "great cold water." You decide.

Either way, this ride presents Kitch-iti-kipi, Michigan's largest spring, found at Palms Book State Park. Forty-five feet deep and 200 feet wide, the spring keeps a constant temperature of 45° F as an incredible 16,000 gallons of water per minute rushes into it.

The other body of water on the ride is Indian Lake, where the route begins at the Indian Lake State Park. Exit the park and head west on CO 442. Birches and pines line the road, which is filled with curves and rolling hills. A paved shoulder makes riding comfortable. Turn right onto CO 455, at 1.5 miles, at the sign for PALMS BOOK STATE PARK.

The hills and curves continue as well as the thick trees on either side of the road. Turn right onto M–149 North at 5.8 miles. Curve left

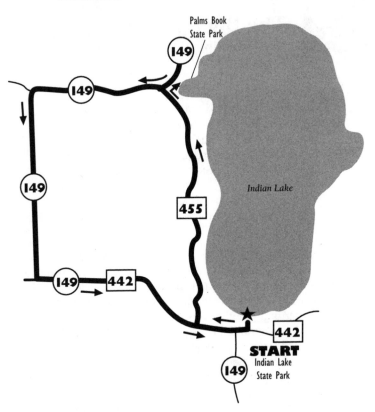

Palms Book
State Park

149

149

149

149

149 442

455

Indian Lake

442

START
Indian Lake
State Park

149

HOW to get there — From Manistique, drive west on CO 442 to Indian Lake State Park.

DIREC-TIONS
at a glance

0.0	From Indian Lake State Park entrance, turn right onto CO 442.
1.5	Turn right onto CO 455.
5.8	Turn right onto M–149 North.
6.6	Curve right into Palms Book State Park.
6.9	Complete loop out of Palms Book State Park and curve left onto M–149 South.
11.4	Stop and turn left onto CO 442, following M–149 South.
14.8	Continue straight on CO 442 as M–149 South turns right.
15.5	Turn left into Indian Lake State Park entrance.

and then right into the Palms Book State Park, at 6.6 miles. It offers picnic tables, drinking water, food, souvenirs, and rest rooms. Find the paved path to the big spring at the end of the parking lot.

A quick ride or walk (the path is narrow and curves sharply among trees) leads you to Kitch-iti-kipi. Along the path are informational panels explaining how this state tourist attraction is really just a sinkhole with a fast-flowing spring. You can see the steep, sloping banks by riding the observation raft at the end of the path. Steel cables guide the raft, which riders themselves must move across the spring. The raft has two "holes" in the middle, affording a view all the way to the bottom of the clear, blue watery depths.

Finish the loop around the parking lot to head south on M–149. From the paved shoulder, experience small rolling hills and curves. At 7.8 miles, curve left and begin a section with diverse wildflowers and grasses. By 10.0 miles, houses take over for the trees, but for less than a mile.

Follow M–149 South (here also known as CO 442), to the left at 11.4 miles. After a hill 0.5 mile later, the road flattens, but the curves continue, along with the trees, grasses, wildflowers, and ferns. At 14.8 miles, follow CO 442 straight when M–149 South turns right. The ride winds down with a nice cattail-filled marsh at 15.2 miles, just 0.3 mile before the turn left into the Indian Lake State Park entrance. Ride through the campground for great views of Indian Lake.

The Au Train Amble:
Santa Claus and Three Waterfalls

Number of miles:	32.7
Approximate pedaling time:	4 hours
Terrain:	Rolling hills, several steep
Traffic:	Moderate
Things to see:	Three waterfalls, sandy beaches of Lake Superior, Lake Au Train, towns of Munising, Au Train, and Christmas
Food:	Restaurants along M–28 and one in Au Train

While riding along M–28 west of Munising, it seems that the view of Lake Superior couldn't get more spectacular—then the next view argues the point. Plenty of roadside parks offer comfortable spots for contemplation of the big lake, as well as breaks from the occasional long and steep hills. Along the way you will see some of the best pines and birches in the state, three wonderful waterfalls, and a town where Santa Claus "reins" supreme each month, not just in December.

Pedal west out of Munising on the sidewalk along the winding Munising Avenue (M–28). At 1.5 miles, move to the street when the road narrows to two lanes with a wide shoulder. Hills begin almost immediately, but there's a payoff at 2.0 miles, with a view of the whole South Bay. Pass roadside parks every 1 or 2 miles; at 2.5 miles, there's an excellent one.

The main attraction, Lake Superior, was so called by the French supposedly not because it's the second-largest lake in the world but for its location north of, or "superior" (meaning above) to, Lake Huron. French explorer Etienne Brulé was one of the first Europeans to travel its shores, around 1622; it was soon used by fur traders and then by ore and grain boats.

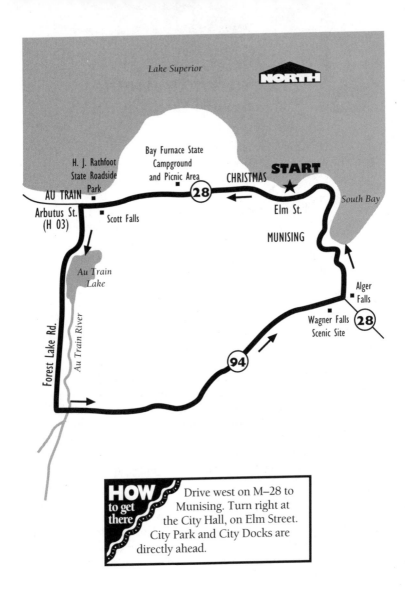

Lake Superior

NORTH

Bay Furnace State Campground and Picnic Area

H. J. Rathfoot State Roadside Park

START

CHRISTMAS

AU TRAIN

28

Arbutus St. (H 03)

Elm St.

Scott Falls

South Bay

MUNISING

Au Train Lake

Alger Falls

Forest Lake Rd.

Au Train River

Wagner Falls Scenic Site

28

94

HOW to get there Drive west on M–28 to Munising. Turn right at the City Hall, on Elm Street. City Park and City Docks are directly ahead.

0.0   From the City Park and City Docks on Lake Superior, ride south on Elm Street and turn right onto Munising Avenue (M–28).

0.9   City Park boat launch.

2.5   Roadside park.

3.3   City picnic area and campgrounds.

3.9   Welcome to Christmas.

4.8   Bay Furnace State Campground and Picnic Area.

9.7   Scott Falls.

10.0   Roadside park.

10.6   Scenic pull-off.

11.2   Turn left onto H 03.

11.3   Town of Au Train. H 03 called Arbutus Street in Au Train; later it becomes Forest Lake Road.

11.9   Doucette Bridge.

12.6   Cameron Crossing and Au Train Lake.

19.0   Stop and turn left onto M–94.

21.8   Ackerman Lake.

24.4   Island Lake National Forest Campground.

30.8   Wagner Falls Scenic Site.

31.2   Stop and turn left onto M–28. At stop, look straight ahead for Alger Falls.

31.9   Railroad crossing.

32.7   Turn right onto Elm Street to City Park and City Docks.

After a flat section, ride into Christmas, at 4.2 miles. Huge reindeer and Santa Clauses adorn the buildings, where decorations and gifts are sold. Leave Saint Nick behind for another wonderful stop at 9.7 miles. At the bottom of a long downhill, find Scott Falls on the left, just before the H. J. Rathfoot State Roadside Park. Water cascades 10 feet into a pool, leaving enough room to walk on the rocks behind the falling water.

Continue riding up and down, curving left and right, and enjoying the lake and trees to H 03, at 11.2 miles. Turn left and immediately cross railroad tracks. On the right is the Au Train Bicycle Shoppe, in case you've forgotten any gear. Then enter Au Train, with its country store, gas station, and restaurant. H 03 snuggles up to Au Train Lake on the left for the first third of the ride on this road, then to the Au Train River for the rest of the way. The road is narrow, but traffic moves slowly through the winding curves. Hills aren't as steep here, so there's time to enjoy the lake peeking through the birches. At 15.4 miles, go past the road to the National Forest Recreational Area. A short 2-mile side trip will take you to an area with toilets and picnic tables.

At 19.0 miles, turn left onto M–94's wide shoulder. Flat sections give you a break between the long hills. As you ride a long downhill, at 26.3 miles, you encounter a wonderful view of the treetops. Continue moving down through curves to Wagner Falls Scenic Site, at 30.8 miles. A short path through deep-green mossy trees and ferns guides you to the falls. Unlike the straight drop of Scott Falls, Wagner Falls is created by water rushing over several rock drops and fallen trees.

The next waterfalls are only 0.5 mile away, at the intersection of M–94 and M–28. At the stop sign look directly ahead to view the Alger Falls, tucked into a part of the hillside. Turn left; the businesses of Munising soon line the road. At 31.8 miles, just before a set of railroad tracks, a road to the right leads to Horseshoe Falls. It's off the route, and a fee is charged to view the privately owned falls, but waterfall buffs would enjoy the 4-block side trip.

At 32.4 miles, you're headed straight for the water until a sharp left curve turns M–28 along the coastline. Encounter the Munising City Hall on Elm Street, at 32.7 miles. Turn right, and the docks and park welcome you back.

The Marquette Amble:
From the Prison to Presque Isle

Number of miles:	29.0 (9.0 for shorter loop)
Approximate pedaling time:	4 hours
Terrain:	Rolling hills, several steep hills
Traffic:	Avoid longer loop at rush hour
Things to see:	Presque Isle Park, Ore Docks, Maritime Museum, lighthouse, Lake Superior coastline, Marquette County Courthouse
Food:	Restaurants in Marquette and Harvey; snacks at Beaver Grove and Crossroads

This ride includes the best of both worlds: The first half travels a favorite route of Marquette cyclists, the second half a favorite of tourists and locals alike. Both present vast vistas of Lake Superior, Marquette landmarks, rolling hills (some steep), and lakeside parks.

Ellwood A. Mattson Lower Harbor Park, the focal point and beginning of both the long and short rides, curves as it hugs the shore of Marquette Bay. It has a wonderful grassy area with picnic tables, a pavilion, drinking water, and rest rooms. Leave the park, riding south along the bay. A short ride on roads through a business section leads to Hampton Street and a ride along the water again. Soon you're on the Lakeside Bike Path along U.S. 41 and M–28 with Lake Superior only feet away.

Pass the prison store, at 2.6 miles, where inmates sell handmade wood and leather items. Continue along the lakeshore until 4.1 miles, where a curve and hill move the route inland. One mile later, M–28 turns left, and the bike path ends. Go across U.S. 41 to ride the wide shoulder over a flat and straight run to CO 480.

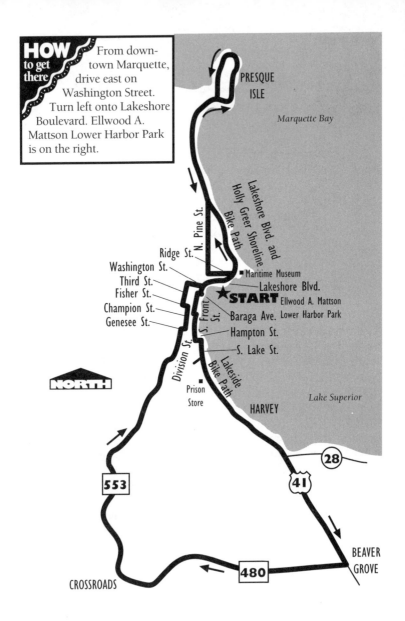

HOW to get there From downtown Marquette, drive east on Washington Street. Turn left onto Lakeshore Boulevard. Ellwood A. Mattson Lower Harbor Park is on the right.

PRESQUE ISLE

Marquette Bay

Lakeshore Blvd. and Holly Greer Shoreline Bike Path

N. Pine St.

Ridge St.

Washington St.

Third St.

Fisher St.

Champion St.

Genesee St.

S. Front St.

Division St.

Maritime Museum

Lakeshore Blvd.

START Ellwood A. Mattson Lower Harbor Park

Baraga Ave.

Hampton St.

S. Lake St.

Lakeside Bike Path

NORTH

Prison Store

Lake Superior

HARVEY

28

41

553

480

BEAVER GROVE

CROSSROADS

DIRECTIONS at a glance

0.0	Turn left out of Ellwood A. Mattson Lower Harbor Park to ride along Lakeshore Boulevard, riding the road or bike path.
0.5	Turn right onto Baraga Avenue and left onto South Front Street.
1.0	Traffic light.
1.2	Turn left onto Hampton Street.
1.3	Curve right; road becomes South Lake Street.
2.3	Road curves right. Turn left to pick up the beginning of bike path. Path follows U.S. 41 and M–28.
2.6	Prison store.
3.7	Welcome Center and rest area.
4.0	Town of Harvey.
4.7	Traffic light.
5.1	At traffic light, M–28 turns left and U.S. 41 continues straight. Bike path ends. Cross road to ride shoulder along U.S. 41.
7.5	Turn right onto CO 480 at Beaver Grove.
12.9	Stop and turn right onto CO 553 at Crossroads.
16.6	Marquette Mountain Ski Area.
18.3	Curve left; road becomes Division Street.
18.7	Curve right onto Genesee Street.
18.8	Turn left onto Champion Street.
19.2	Stop and turn left onto Fisher Street.
19.3	Stop and turn right onto Third Street.
19.4	Flashing yellow light at Baraga Avenue; Marquette County Courthouse follows.
19.5	Railroad tracks.
19.6	Turn right onto Washington Street.
19.7	Traffic light.
19.75	Stop and turn left onto Lakeshore Boulevard.
20.0	Pass entrance to Ellwood A. Mattson Lower Harbor Park. (Shorter option begins here.)
20.2	Road curves sharply left. Turn right to pick up beginning of Holly Greer Shoreline Bike Path on Coast Guard Road. Maritime Museum here.

20.25 Railroad crossing.

20.3 Coast Guard lighthouse.

20.4 Path crosses McCarty Cove Park parking lot.

20.9 Picnic Rocks at Shiras Park.

21.6 Stop and cross road to follow path.

22.6 Dead River Park with falls and drinking fountain.

23.0 Ore dock on right.

23.1 Railroad crossing, followed by Presque Isle Park. Enter here.

23.2 Path ends at gravel parking lot. Ride through parking lot and turn right to pick up park road.

23.3 Veer right at Y onto one-way road; a breakwall soon follows.

23.6 Turn right to rejoin one-way main park road.

25.5 Veer right to exit Presque Isle Park.

25.6 Veer right onto bike path along Lakeshore Boulevard.

25.7 Railroad crossing.

27.2 Continue straight on bike path along North Pine Street as another branch of path veers left to follow Lakeshore Boulevard.

27.5 Railroad crossing.

27.6 *Use caution* at flashing yellow light and continue straight across East Fair Avenue. Bike path moves onto sidewalk. Ride the road.

28.1 *Use caution* at blinking light at intersection with East Hewitt Avenue.

28.4 Stop as North Pine Street dead-ends into Ridge Street East. Turn left.

28.8 Stop and turn right onto Lakeshore Boulevard.

29.0 Turn left into Ellwood A. Mattson Lower Harbor Park parking lot.

9.0 miles

0.0 Turn right out of Ellwood A. Mattson Lower Harbor Park onto Lakeshore Boulevard. Follow directions for longer loop beginning at 20.0 miles.

Turn right, and the wide shoulders will give you plenty of room to navigate the long hills and curves. Pass creeks, enormous pine trees, white birches, and colorful wildflowers on the way to Crossroads, the junction with CO 553. Turn right and begin the section of long, steep curvy downs and ups. Pass the Marquette Mountain Ski Area just before a steep uphill, at 16.6 miles. The hardest work is over as the road begins to flatten a mile later.

At 18.0 miles, houses sprout up along the road. Downtown arrives several turns later and the Marquette County Courthouse at 19.4 miles. The sandstone, domed courthouse, built in neoclassical revival style from 1902 to 1904, was the setting of the 1959 film *Anatomy of a Murder*. Inspired by a case tried here, the late Ishpeming author John D. Voelker wrote the novel on which the movie was based.

Head east toward the water to connect with Lakeshore Boulevard. Ride past Mattson Park, where the shorter option joins the route. As the road curves left, the Holly Greer Shoreline Bike Path begins on the right, forming a wedge for the Maritime Museum. Housed in a beautiful red-brick building, it offers self-guided tours through the displays of old boats and marine hardware and information on lumber hookers, topsail schooners, and Mackinac boats.

Continue on the path past the U.S. Coast Guard Station and the Marquette Lighthouse, at 20.3 miles. The bike path winds its way along the coastline, moving through parks and past sandy and rocky beaches on the way to Presque Isle. Although the name means "almost an island," the 328-acre Presque Isle has a lot—tall cliffs overlooking Lake Superior, nature trails, a bog walk, picnic areas, and "wild" deer that approach you looking for a tasty apple or other treats. Ride around the isle on a hilly, one-way road that presents dramatic views of Lake Superior.

On the return to Mattson Park, follow the bike path back to the intersection of North Pine Street. Veer right and ride the path along Pine Street for a ride through a quiet residential area. (If you prefer the water, veer left and backtrack to the park.) When the path ends, at 27.6 miles, switch to the road. Turn left onto Ridge Street for a high panoramic view of Marquette Bay before turning onto Lakeshore Boulevard and completing the ride.

A Superior Ride:
Copper Harbor and
Brockway Mountain Drive

Number of miles:	21.6
Approximate pedaling time:	4 hours
Terrain:	Hills, many steep
Traffic:	Light to moderate on holiday weekends
Things to see:	Sweeping Lake Superior vistas, Brockway Mountain Drive, Fort Wilkins Historic Complex and Michigan State Park
Food:	Restaurants in Copper Harbor; snacks only at West Bluff Scenic View and Fort Wilkins State Park

One of the most spectacular rides in the book, this is also one of the most challenging, but you receive a great payoff for the effort. Located in northern Keweenaw Peninsula, M–26 has one scenic view after another of the Lake Superior coastline, varying from white sugary beaches to red rocky outcrops. As if that isn't enough, the second half of the ride encompasses Brockway Mountain Drive, which has been called the best scenic drive in the state and one of the most picturesque drives in the Midwest.

Ride south on wide U.S. 41 as you leave the Fort Wilkins Historic Complex and Michigan State Park, on Lake Fanny Hooe. The park offers a look at a nineteenth-century military post. In the spring watch for hawks, as the state park is on their migration route. Eagles and owls also fly in the area.

Begin winding up and down small humps. Here, as is the case throughout the ride, birches, pine trees, grasses, and wildflowers line the road. Lake Superior peeks through the trees just before you ride into the town of Copper Harbor. Restaurants and gift shops selling pieces of copper from the area border the road.

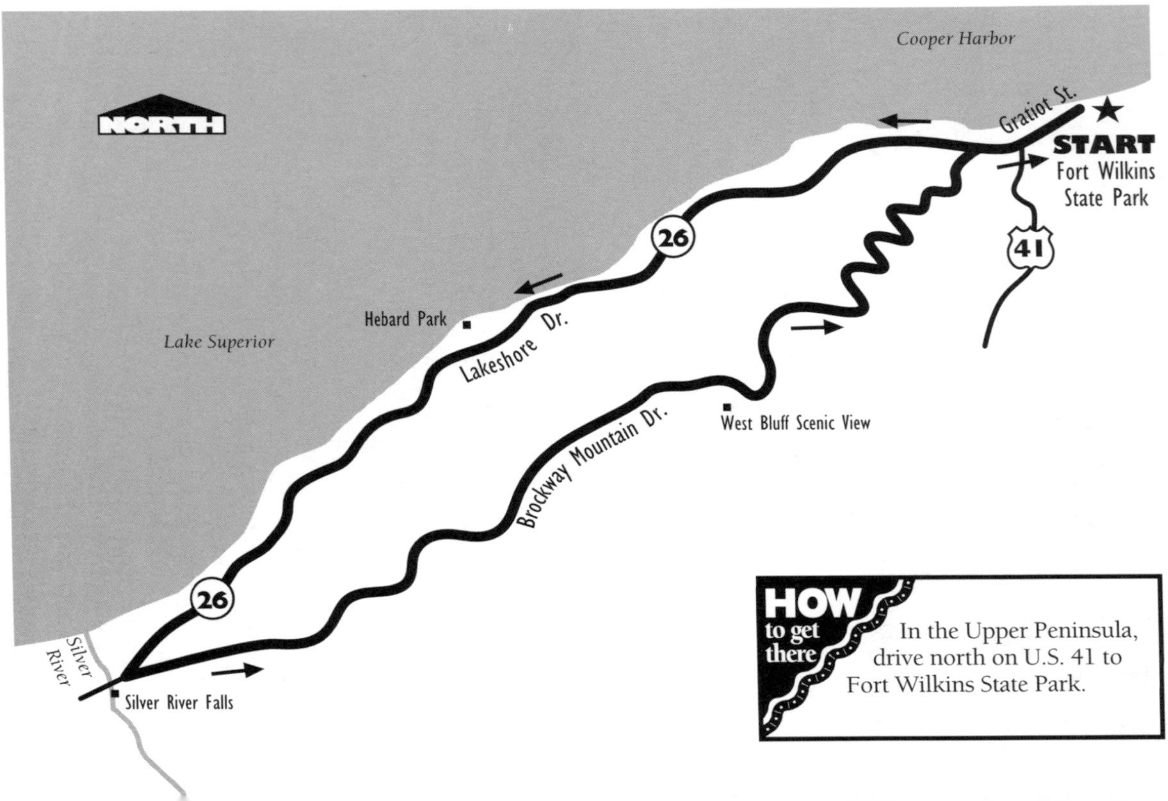

NORTH

Cooper Harbor

Lake Superior

Gratiot J.

START
Fort Wilkins State Park

41

26

West Bluff Scenic View

Brockway Mountain Dr.

Lakeshore Dr.

Hebard Park

26

Silver River Falls

Silver River

HOW to get there

In the Upper Peninsula, drive north on U.S. 41 to Fort Wilkins State Park.

DIREC- TIONS
at a glance

0.0	Turn left onto U.S. 41, leaving Fort Wilkins State Park.
1.2	Copper Harbor. The road is called Gratiot Street in town; it later changes to Lakeshore Drive.
1.5	Continue straight onto M–26 as U.S. 41 turns left.
1.6	Copper Harbor Marina.
4.2	Hebard Park.
10.7	Turn left onto Brockway Mountain Drive. (*Option:* Continue straight a few yards to see Silver River Falls before returning to ride Brockway Mountain Drive.)
15.7	West Bluff Scenic View.
19.7	Stop and turn right onto M–26.
20.2	Continue straight as U.S. 41 joins M–26.
21.6	Turn right into Fort Wilkins State Park.

At 1.5 miles, U.S. 41 turns left, but the ride continues straight on M–26, the road to Eagle Harbor. After the intersection, curves and rolling hills begin in earnest. A good opportunity to pull off the road comes at 3.9 miles, where the blue water splashes against red rocks. Hebard Park, 0.3 mile later, has a great view, picnic tables, and toilets. Continue up and down, curving left and right to another roadside park, at 9.7 miles. Steps cut into the red rocks lead to a lake overlook.

The turn onto Brockway Mountain Drive comes at 10.7 miles. Before you turn, however, you may want to ride a few extra yards to see the Silver River and its falls. On the right are steps leading down to the falls; on the left, past the bridge, are picnic tables. Head back and make the turn onto the drive.

Brockway Mountain Drive reaches 735 feet above Lake Superior and 1,300 feet above sea level, so you know what you're in for. Actually, most of the ride up has hills, with areas of flat to catch your breath. The ride down does have very steep hills, so brakes should be in the best repair.

Begin with an immediate uphill on this wide, sun-dappled road. At 14.6 miles, look right through the trees for a glimpse of the valley below. By 15.5 miles, Lake Superior can be seen glistening on the left. Just 0.2 mile later, veer right to stop at the West Bluff Scenic View. It has a map of the Keweenaw Harbor, with information on the history of copper mining. The Skytop Inn has gifts and candy but nothing to drink, as electricity is not available.

Return to the Y, and start the downhill run. The drive has signs posted before each steep downhill. Scenic overlooks for the bluffs continue all the way down, offering good spots to rest your brake hand and admire the lake.

At 19.6 miles, ride up a hill, curve left, and you're at M–26. Turn right, and pass the marina, the junction of U.S. 41, and Copper Harbor on the way back. At 21.6 miles, turn right into Fort Wilkins State Park, completing a most dramatic ride.

A Grand Ride at Presque Isle

Number of miles:	27.4
Approximate pedaling time:	4 hours
Terrain:	Rolling hills
Traffic:	Can be heavy on U.S. 23
Things to see:	Presque Isle and Old Presque Isle lighthouses, Grand Lake, vistas of Lake Huron
Food:	Gas stations at 8.4 and 12.6 miles; general store and restaurants at 16.4 miles; and general store at 22.0 miles

Not one but two lighthouses decorate this ride filled with vistas of Lake Huron and Grand Lake. Also on the route is the Besser Natural Area, and great riding over country roads with rolling hills.

Unload your bike at the Besser Natural Area. Before or after the ride, stretch your legs on the one-mile trail that winds through the woods and is filled with huge virgin white pines, a spot of unspoiled Lake Huron coastline, a lagoon, and the ghost town of Bell. Many people visit the area for this walk alone.

When your legs are warmed up, hop on the bike and turn left from Besser Bell Trail onto Grand Lake Road. Traffic is light on this road filled with curves, trees, and wildflowers. The route straightens after 0.8 mile, but remains mostly flat. At 2.9 miles, turn right onto U.S. 23—it can be busy but has a wide shoulder. At 3.5 miles, a gentle curve to the left unveils a view of Grand Lake through the trees.

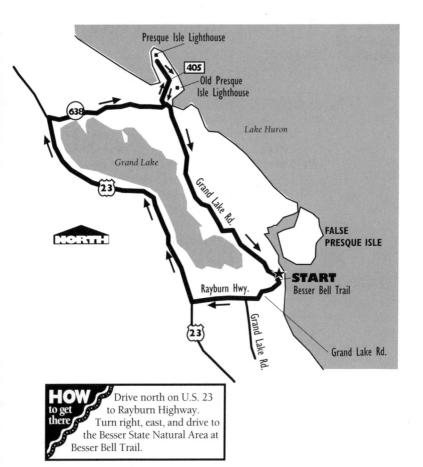

Presque Isle Lighthouse

405

Old Presque
Isle Lighthouse

638

Lake Huron

Grand Lake

23

NORTH

Grand Lake Rd.

FALSE
PRESQUE ISLE

START
Besser Bell Trail

Rayburn Hwy.

23

Grand Lake Rd.

Grand Lake Rd.

HOW to get there Drive north on U.S. 23 to Rayburn Highway. Turn right, east, and drive to the Besser State Natural Area at Besser Bell Trail.

DIREC-TIONS at a glance

0.0 From Besser Bell Trail, turn left onto Grand Lake Road.

0.8 Continue straight at intersection as Grand Lake Road turns left.

2.9 Stop and turn right onto U.S. 23.

11.6 Turn right onto CO 638.

13.8 Turn left to follow CO 638.

15.8 Stop and turn left onto Grand Lake Road, CO 405.

16.7 Old Presque Isle Lighthouse.

17.5 Enter parking lot of Presque Isle Lighthouse.

17.8 Leave parking lot.

18.7 Old Presque Isle Lighthouse.

19.6 Continue straight to ride Grand Lake Road.

27.4 Turn left to return to Besser Bell Trail.

Begin a long, easy uphill at 5.5 miles and enjoy another great peek at the lake. Within 2 miles you've ridden up to a treetop view of the lake. More hills bring you to lakeside parks at 8.0 and 10.1 miles.

Turn right onto CO 638 at 11.6 miles, a wide road with plenty of room to ride. Small pines and birches hide the houses along the way. The lake comes back into view again after a curve at 12.3 miles, with a great spot for a break alongside the lake 0.1 mile later.

Curves continue on CO 638, as well as CO 405, Grand Lake Road. Lake Huron makes a dramatic appearance at 16.1 miles; a marina and a cluster of businesses soon follow. At 16.7 miles, the short road to the Old Presque Isle Lighthouse and Museum is on the right. Completed in 1840, this is one of the oldest lighthouses currently on the Great Lakes. It's open to the public for a small fee.

Less than a mile later is the second lighthouse on the ride. It was completed in 1870 and is one of the tallest on the lakes. The lighthouse tower rises from a limestone foundation to reach 113 feet—and it's open to interested climbers. (The view of the coastline from the top is incredible.) Picnic tables, rest rooms, grills, a pop machine, and a gift shop can be found here.

Backtrack from the lighthouse to the intersection of Grand Lake Road and CO 638. Continue riding on Grand Lake Road; it's mostly flat here with plenty of curves and a small shoulder. Pass the Presque Isle community at 21.5 miles, and the John Kauffman Homestead, a Michigan historic site, at 21.9 miles.

Glimpse Grand Lake at 22.0 miles, as trees replace houses and the trees move closer to the road. Curves continue to 26.9 miles where they're interrupted by a straight stretch and a small but long uphill. When you pass Bell Bay Road on the left, you're on the last few curves of the ride. At 27.4 miles, turn left onto Besser Bell Trail and return to the land of the giant pines.

ERECTED TO PERPETUATE THE MEMORY OF THE
PIONEER LUMBERMEN OF MICHIGAN THROUGH
WHOSE LABORS WAS MADE POSSIBLE THE
DEVELOPMENT OF THE PRAIRIE STATES

Awesome Au Sable Amble

Number of miles:	32.5
Approximate pedaling time:	4 hours
Terrain:	Rolling hills
Traffic:	Light
Things to see:	River Road National Forest Scenic Byway, Lumberman's Monument, Iargo Springs, Au Sable River
Food:	The Dam Store and Old Orchard Campground

Approximately 14 miles of this ride wind along River Road National Forest Scenic Byway, one of only ninety-eight designated scenic byways in the country. It's easy to see why this route would be chosen as a byway. River Road runs parallel to the southern bank of the mighty Au Sable River. Along the route on this road are great vistas, the Lumberman's Monument, Iargo Springs, parts of the Huron National Forest, and the Canoers' Memorial Monument.

Twenty-two miles in length, River Road National Forest Scenic Byway begins in Oscoda on River Road and ends on M–65, 5 miles north of Hale. This ride begins at one of the highlights of the River Road: Lumberman's Monument Visitors Center. Here are drinking water, rest rooms, covered tables, footpaths, Au Sable River scenic overlooks, and a camping area. The monument to the lumbermen has three 9-foot-high bronze figures: a sawyer, with ax and saw; a river driver, with peavey; and a timber cruiser, with compass. These and many more lumber terms are explained along the interpretive path at the Visitors Center.

Leaving the center and riding west on River Road, the route fea-

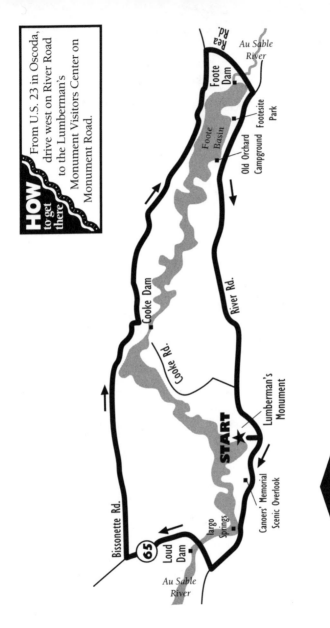

HOW to get there

From U.S. 23 in Oscoda, drive west on River Road to the Lumberman's Monument Visitors Center on Monument Road.

Au Sable River

Rea Rd.

Foote Dam

Footesite Park

Foote Basin

Old Orchard Campground

Cooke Dam

Cooke Rd.

River Rd.

Lumberman's Monument

START

Canoers' Memorial Scenic Overlook

Bissonette Rd.

Iargo Springs

65

Loud Dam

Au Sable River

NORTH

DIRECTIONS
at a glance

0.0 Leave parking area of the Lumberman's Monument Visitors Center via Monument Road.
0.2 Turn right onto River Road.
1.5 Canoers' Memorial Scenic Overlook.
2.9 Iargo Springs Interpretive Area.
3.9 Stop and turn right onto M–65.
6.8 Turn right onto Bissonette Road.
20.9 Turn right onto Rea Road
22.2 Foote Dam.
22.7 Stop and turn right onto River Road.
23.0 Footesite Park.
24.9 Old Orchard Campground.
32.3 Turn right onto Lumberman's Monument Road into Visitors Center.
32.5 Parking area.

tures rolling hills, forests, and a paved shoulder. At 1.5 miles is the Canoers' Memorial Monument, dedicated to all those who brave the Au Sable River, especially those who participate in the annual canoe race. Look for eagles nesting.

After more small hills, trees, and curves, at 2.9 miles is Iargo Springs, what the locals consider the most beautiful spot on the Scenic Byway. Ride into the parking area and enjoy the panoramic view of the river from the 30-foot-high observation deck, or walk down the almost 300 steps to the springs themselves. For hundreds of years Indians met here. It's not hard to understand why—water filters down through the ground and emerges to join the river. From the moisture, trees, grasses, and ferns put on a show of every shade of green imaginable.

Climb back up the steps. Now your legs are warmed up and ready for more hills on River Road. Turn right onto M–65 and enjoy a wide shoulder and more rolling hills. At 4.7 miles, the road crosses the Au Sable River; Loud Dam is on the left. The road loses the curves at 5.1 miles; it flattens a mile later. A right turn onto Bissonette Road offers a wide, curvy street with light traffic and beautiful trees. The river, which has been hidden by trees, reappears at 10.7 miles.

Bissonette Road eventually straightens and flattens before the right turn onto Rea Road. This road, too, is flat and wide. A mile after the turn, Foote Dam is on the right as the route crosses the river. At the corner of Rea and River Roads are several stores and restaurants, with The Dam Store on the corner. Soon the *River Queen* commands the view, offering cruises on the waterway. Footesite Park is just past this, at 23.0 miles, with drinking water, river access, and rest rooms.

The last leg of the ride begins straight, but as the end of the ride approaches, River Road has more curves. Old Orchard Campground, at 24.9 miles, has a store for supplies. Just before the return to Lumberman's Monument, on the right, is Cooke Road, which leads to Cooke Dam (for those who have the energy for a longer ride). A right turn onto Lumberman's Monument Road, at 32.3 miles, leads back to the Visitors Center and one last look at the mighty Au Sable.

Two Tawases and a Beach

Number of miles:	25 (14.2 for shorter loop)
Approximate pedaling time:	3 hours
Terrain:	Mostly flat
Traffic:	Low, except on U.S. 23 and M–55, which can be heavy
Things to see:	Tawas Point, historic lighthouse, scenic views of Lake Huron, towns of Tawas City and East Tawas
Food:	Many options along U.S. 23

For this ride's fantastic scenery, give the credit to Lake Huron and Tawas Bay. Some credit must also go to Tawas City and East Tawas for making it easy to enjoy. A 7-mile-long lighted bike path follows the shoreline of Tawas Bay through Tawas City and East Tawas on its way to Tawas Point State Park. Along the path are parks, lake accesses, the county museum, and a historic lighthouse.

The other part of the ride, off the path, is no slouch on the scenery either: Tawas River, rolling hills, farms, and marshes. Begin at the state park, visiting the Tawas Point Lighthouse before or after the ride. The main road in the park leads to a lighthouse built in 1876, still used by the Coast Guard today and open for touring.

Heading north out of the state park, the bike path alongside the road begins at 0.6 mile. The view of the lake is quickly lost, blocked by tall trees along the curves of Tawas Beach Road. More of Lake Huron is visible after a turn onto Baldwin Resort Road. There's no bike path here, but the road has little traffic, and what traffic there is moves slowly through the curves.

Traffic moves quickly on U.S. 23, but the road's wide shoulder

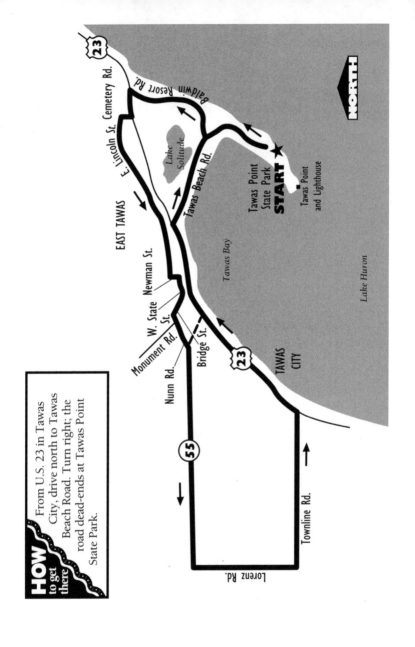

HOW to get there

From U.S. 23 in Tawas City, drive north to Tawas Beach Road. Turn right; the road dead-ends at Tawas Point State Park.

NORTH

23

Cemetery Rd.

E. Lincoln St.

Baldwin Resort Rd.

Lake Solitude

EAST TAWAS

Tawas Beach Rd.

Newman St.

W. State St.

Monument Rd.

Nunn Rd.

Bridge St.

55

23

TAWAS CITY

Townline Rd.

Lorenz Rd.

Tawas Bay

Tawas Point State Park

START

Tawas Point and Lighthouse

Lake Huron

DIREC-TIONS at a glance

0.0 Leave Tawas Point State Park via Tawas Beach Road.

0.6 Bike path begins on west side of road.

1.3 Cross road from bike path and turn right onto Baldwin Resort Road.

3.6 Stop, cross, and then turn left onto U.S. 23.

5.7 Turn right onto Cemetery Road and *use caution* at immediate railroad crossing.

5.8 Stop and turn left onto East Lincoln Street.

7.3 Turn left onto Newman Street.

7.4 Turn right onto West State Street.

7.8 Curve right onto Bridge Street; bike lane begins.

8.1 Bike lane continues across bridge.

8.3 Road curves left at Monument Road and becomes Nunn Road.

8.9 Stop and turn right onto West M–55.

13.0 Turn left onto Lorenz Road.

14.1 Continue straight after four-way stop.

15.1 Turn left onto Townline Road.

17.7 Railroad crossing.

18.1 Cross U.S. 23 and turn left onto the beginning of bike path.

22.2 Turn right onto Tawas Beach Road.

25.0 Return to Tawas Point State Park entrance.

14.2 miles

0.0 Follow the longer loop to the intersection of Nunn Road and M–55.

8.9 Turn left onto East M–55.

9.2 Cross Tawas River.

9.5 Railroad tracks.

9.6 Stop and turn left onto U.S. 23, joining longer loop.

11.4 Turn right onto Tawas Beach Road.

14.2 Return to Tawas Point State Park entrance.

makes riding enjoyable. Turns onto Cemetery Road and East Lincoln Street put the route into a quiet residential area. Don't miss the old church on Newman Street, at 7.3 miles. The turn here leads to the business section of East Tawas. At 7.4 miles, continue straight if you'd like a side trip to see the shops, or follow the route and turn right onto West State Street. On this corner is another wonderful building—red brick and built in 1887.

Cross the Tawas River to the intersection of M–55. Wide shoulders makes this a good road to ride even though it's busy. The scenery as well as the terrain change on Lorenz and Townline Roads, from flat with trees, to hills, fields, and marshes. Crossing U.S. 23 brings the ride to the bike path along Tawas Bay. Pass City Hall and Gateway Park, at 19.2 miles. Gateway Park has drinking water, rest rooms, and picnic tables, and it's a great place to admire the bay.

At 20.5 miles are the Chamber of Commerce and the Iosco County Historical Museum. And 0.7 mile later is City Park, which has drinking water, rest rooms, and picnic tables. Many restaurants and stores line U.S. 23, offering food and supplies.

The bike path swings right onto Tawas Beach Road, at 22.2 miles. Along the way the path switches from a bike lane to a bike path, and then back to a bike lane. With the thick trees on both sides of the road, it feels like a forest. At 24.6 miles, cottages and a marina take over for the trees before Tawas Bay and Lake Huron dominate the scenery at the state park.

The shorter loop includes great lake vistas and a tour of the business district. You'll miss the rolling hills, fields, and marshes of the longer ride, but the loop includes the wonderful bike paths along Tawas Bay and Tawas Beach Road. Both paths are unsurpassed in their natural beauty.

The Tip o' Thumb Tour

Number of miles:	24.9 (11.6 for shorter loop)
Approximate pedaling time:	3 hours
Terrain:	Rolling hills
Traffic:	Can be heavy on M–25
Things to see:	Historic Huron City and Grindstone City; Pointe aux Barques Lighthouse and Museum; sweeping Lake Huron vistas
Food:	In town of Port Austin; Grindstone Bar, 5.2 miles; Danny Zeb's, 5.7 miles

The best way to explore the many attractions of Michigan's "thumb" area is on a bike. And this route covers them all: a ghost town, a lighthouse and museum, sandy beaches, the home of the grindstone, and more. Start this ride in Port Austin, a quiet, lakeside community that rests at the very tip of the thumb.

From the marina and public access, head east on wide Spring Street, which later becomes Pointe aux Barques Road. The road narrows at 0.5 mile, but light traffic and low speeds make it a nice ride. You will wind past farms and trees and over creeks, with wildflowers lining the way. Get ready for a long uphill from 2.8 to 3.2 miles. At 3.4 miles, there's a big downhill, with trees rushing past.

At 5.0 miles, stop and turn left, following the road. Before pedaling off, look straight ahead to see the first grindstone on the ride. Curve right at 5.2 miles to find the Grindstone Bar; Lake Huron is on the left. Just after the Harbor Marina, at 5.4 miles, a grindstone rests in a yard on the right. Watch for others in this area, left from the days when the people of Grindstone City used the local sandstone to pro-

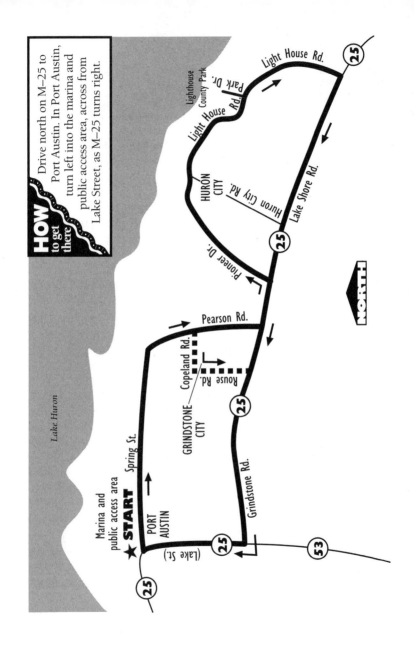

DIRECTIONS at a glance

0.0 From traffic light at entrance to the marina and public access, turn left onto Spring Street.

5.0 Turn left, following road.

5.6 Make hard right; road becomes Pearson Road.

5.8 Go straight past Copeland Road. (*Option:* Shorter loop turns right.)

6.2 Stop and turn left onto M–25, Grindstone Road.

8.8 Turn left onto Pioneer Drive.

9.6 Pass Huron City Road.

9.8 Turn left onto Light House Road.

11.4 Road curves right.

12.0 Turn left onto Park Drive to Lighthouse County Park. Leave Lighthouse Park via Park Drive.

12.6 Turn left onto Light House Road to leave the park.

13.4 Turn right onto Lake Shore Road, M–25 north.

24.5 Stop and turn right following M–25 (also called Lake Street).

24.9 Traffic light. Continue straight to marina and public access area.

11.6 miles

0.0 Begin ride by following directions for longer loop.

5.8 Turn right onto Copeland Road to ride to Grindstone City.

6.3 Turn left onto Rouse Road after passing through Grindstone City.

6.6 Turn right onto M–25. Follow longer-loop directions back to Port Austin.

11.6 Return to marina and public access area.

duce grindstones, weighing from 3 pounds to 6 tons, and exported them around the world.

After a hard right, at 5.6 miles, the road becomes Pearson Road. Then 0.2 mile later, the short loop turns right onto Copeland Road to Grindstone City. It has a country store and a grindstone memorial to the city's founders.

The longer loop continues straight to M–25. Turn left and enjoy a wonderful flat and curvy ride on a wide shoulder, including a bridge over a quiet creek. Another left, onto Pioneer Drive, begins the cruise into Huron City, at 9.4 miles. Tours and rest rooms are available at this ghost-town-turned-attraction. Once the largest town in the area, filled with people exploiting timber, it was all changed by a large fire that swept the area in 1881. The town has been preserved to serve as a museum.

Past Huron City, just after a hill, turn left onto Light House Road, at 9.8 miles. Winding downhill through trees brings you closer to Lake Huron, with an especially nice view at 11.4 miles. The road curves right; Lighthouse County Park is in front, the lake on the left. Take Park Drive to explore the lighthouse museum and the park, which has picnic tables, drinking water, and rest rooms.

Winding east on Light House Road, look behind you for a sweeping view of Lake Huron, at 12.9 miles. Then, at 13.4 miles, turn right onto Lake Shore Road, M–25 north. Once again you're on wide shoulders through mostly flat country, except for long uphills at 15.2 and 20.0 miles. Old brick houses and weather-worn barns provide the scenery. M–25 becomes Grindstone Road before entering the Port Austin village limits.

Stop and turn right to stay on M–25 (Lake Street) at 24.5 miles. Wide lanes take you past a spot that offers carriage rides: the Garfield Inn, with its beautiful gardens and house, where James Garfield, later a U.S. president, once stayed; and the Manor Inn, another beautiful red-brick bed and breakfast. At 12.6 miles, at Spring and Lake Streets, ride straight through the intersection to return to glorious Lake Huron views.

Inside the Thumb:
Caseville and the Lake Huron Loop

Number of miles:	23.4 (14.1 for shorter loop)
Approximate pedaling time:	3 hours
Terrain:	Flat, with some hills
Traffic:	Can be heavy on M–25
Things to see:	Panoramic views of Lake Huron coast-line, Caseville and Oak Beach County Parks, Albert E. Sleeper State Park
Food:	Country stores, 0.2, 0.6, and 4.4 miles; gas station at Gotts Corners, 15.2 miles; Caseville; restaurant, 21.8 miles

The Lake Huron coastline stars in this ride—mile after mile of white sugary beaches. Plenty of parks along the way offer spots for picnics and rest breaks. There are also farms, fields, barns, and stately old houses before more coast riding.

Begin at Albert E. Sleeper State Park, with beach access, drinking water, rest rooms, and picnic tables among the trees. Leave the state park riding north on M–25—a perfect road for riding, with its wide shoulder. Traffic may become heavy at times, but the shoulder offers plenty of room.

After leaving the state park, the shorter option turns almost immediately onto State Park Road. Continuing straight, pass country stores, at 0.2 and 0.6 miles. There's beach access at a small park on the left, at 1.0 mile. This section has superb views of Lake Huron, broken only by quaint cottages and trees. A cool breeze from the lake makes for great riding even on the hottest days.

At 2.3 miles, curve right; the view here is spectacular. Pass a scenic turnout at 4.0 miles. A good rest stop is Oak Beach County

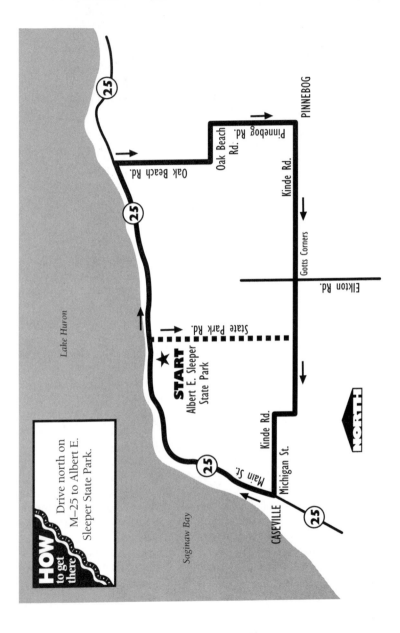

DIREC-TIONS at a glance

0.0 From Albert E. Sleeper State Park, ride north on M–25.

0.2 State Park Road. Continue straight.(*Option:* Shorter loop turns right.)

4.0 Scenic turnout.

4.4 Turn right onto Oak Beach Road.

7.5 Turn right onto Pinnebog Road.

9.5 Stop and turn right onto Kinde Road.

13.5 Four-way stop at Elkton Road.

14.5 State Park Road on right. (Shorter loop rejoins ride.)

16.7 Stop and turn left to remain on Kinde Road. Eastbound traffic does not stop.

17.8 Caseville city limits. Kinde Road becomes Michigan Street.

18.3 Stop and turn right onto M–25 North (Main Street).

23.4 Return to Albert E. Sleeper State Park.

14.1 miles

0.0 Turn north onto M–25 from the state park.

0.2 Turn right onto State Park Road.

5.2 Stop and turn right onto Kinde Road. Follow longer-loop directions from mile 14.5 through Caseville and back to Albert E. Sleeper State Park.

Park, on the left at the turn onto Oak Beach Road. It features trees, white beaches, pavilions, rest rooms, and drinking water.

Oak Beach Road begins with dense trees on both sides. Although it has no shoulder, the traffic is sparse and moves slowly. At 4.6 miles, pass the Huron County Nature Center and Wilderness Arboretum. Soon the trees disappear; flat farmland takes their place.

A sharp curve left, at 6.5 miles, followed by an uphill signals a turn right onto Pinnebog Road. Enjoy a long and easy uphill and downhill, as well as a beautiful creek at 6.7 miles. At the intersection of Pinnebog and Kinde Roads, look left to see some wonderful old

buildings from when Pinnebog was a town. An old Pepsi sign adorns a closed country store.

Head west on Kinde Road's small shoulder for more fields and farms and rolling hills. Watch for some stately old brick houses. Then ride a long uphill. At the top, the road once again is mostly flat with views of farmland.

At 13.5 miles, coast into Gotts Corners. There are more old buildings here as well as a gas station, on the left, for cold drinks and snacks. Cross State Park Road, where the shorter loop joins the longer route, at 14.5 miles. Continue on, *using caution* at 16.7 miles, where the route turns left to remain on Kinde Road. Eastbound traffic does not stop.

A tunnel of trees covers the route at 16.8 miles. Cross a creek, pedal a small uphill, then ride straight and flat and soon you will see a big blue fish on a watertower, welcoming you to Caseville. Turn right onto M–25 into Caseville, with its stores and shops. Here again the road is wide, with plenty of room for bikes and traffic. Cross the Pigeon River, at 18.7 miles, and pass a beautiful church, at 18.8 miles. As you move out of town, at 19.0 miles, the Caseville County Park has drinking water, rest rooms, and more picnic areas on Lake Huron's coastline.

Continue on the wide shoulder past trees on both sides, at 19.4 miles. Breeze along on a mostly flat ride, through curves, past cottages, with lake views through trees. The road hugs the shore all the way back to Albert E. Sleeper State Park.

R & R in Bay City:
The Riverwalk and Rail-Trail Tour

Number of miles:	11.4
Approximate pedaling time:	1½ hours
Terrain:	Mostly flat
Traffic:	Can be busy on Cass Avenue
Things to see:	Saginaw River, Bay City Riverwalk and Rail-Trail, old homes in quiet residential area
Food:	All along route

Bay City's Riverwalk and Rail-Trail highlight this ride. Starting on the riverwalk, the route runs along the bank of the Saginaw River, tours residential areas, and picks up the rail-trail, on the east side of town, before heading back to the river. The riverwalk and rail-trail will eventually be connected, forming a 9-mile-long bike path circling the city, but until then, riders can enjoy a route encompassing the quiet, wide, tree-lined roads between the two.

Begin on the riverwalk, along the west bank of the Saginaw River, by the boat and launch parking area. Depending on the particular summer weekend, there might be fireworks, boat races, or tall ships on the river. The boardwalk features markers giving the history of sawmills and the lumber trade in the area.

On the left, at 0.7 mile, turn onto a beautiful wood-plank bridge for bikes and pedestrians that meanders left and right as it crosses the river. Take a quick break in the middle of the river and enjoy the view. As you leave the bridge, veer right, alongside the water, and follow the path under the overpass.

After the overpass, ride left as the path returns alongside the road. At 1.5 miles, ride the sidewalk bike path as you cross the river once

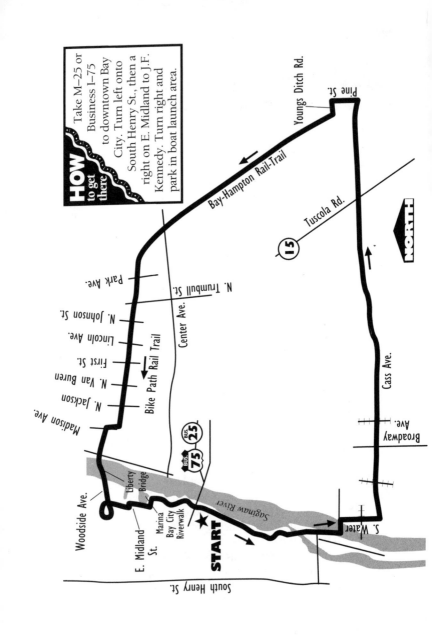

HOW to get there

Take M–25 or Business I–75 to downtown Bay City. Turn left onto South Henry St., then a right on E. Midland to J.F. Kennedy. Turn right and park in boat launch area.

Pine St.

Youngs Ditch Rd.

Bay-Hampton Rail-Trail

Tuscola Rd.

15

NORTH

Park Ave.

N. Trumbull St.

N. Johnson St.

Lincoln Ave.

First St.

N. Van Buren

N. Jackson

Madison Ave.

Center Ave.

Bike Path Rail Trail

Cass Ave.

Broadway Ave.

Woodside Ave.

Liberty Bridge

E. Midland St.

Marina Bay City Riverwalk

Saginaw River

BUS. 75

BUS. 25

S. Water

START

South Henry St.

DIREC- TIONS at a glance

0.0	From the middle bridge over the riverwalk, ride south, keeping river on left.
0.3	Turn left, following path onto bridge.
0.4	Veer left onto wooden bridge. Curve right, then left over another bridge.
0.6	Pier on left; no bikes allowed.

0.7 Take first wood-plank bridge to left. Ride bridge over river.

1.0 Bear right onto sidewalk and ride path close to river.

1.3 Curve right and follow path under overpass.

1.4 Follow path back to road.

1.5 Ride sidewalk bike path to cross river.

1.6 At bottom of bridge, turn immediately right onto South Water.

2.1 Road curves and becomes Harrison Street. *Caution:* Harrison Street and Cass Avenue have sewer grates.

2.4 Railroad crossing.

2.6 Turn left onto Cass Avenue.

3.0 Traffic light at corner of Broadway and Cass Avenues.

3.1 Railroad crossing.

3.4 Traffic light.

5.5 Stop and *use caution* to cross busy South M–15 and then northbound M–15, called Tuscola Road.

5.9 Turn left at blinking light onto Pine Street.

6.9 At four-way stop, turn left onto Youngs Ditch Road.

7.1 Turn right onto Bay-Hampton Rail-Trail.

7.6 Stop and cross road.

7.8 Stop and cross road.

8.0 Stop and cross railroad tracks.

8.4 Stop and cross Center Avenue.

8.5 Caution sign at road crossing.

9.0 Stop and cross Park Avenue.

9.2 Stop and cross North Trumbull Street.

9.4 Stop and cross North Johnson Street.

9.6 Stop and cross Lincoln Avenue.

9.7 Stop and cross First Street.

9.9   Stop and cross North Van Buren.

10.0   Stop and cross North Jackson.

10.1   Stop and turn right onto Madison Avenue.

10.2   Turn left onto Woodside Avenue.

10.6   Ride across Liberty Bridge on the bike path; no bicycles allowed on sidewalk. Traffic light in middle of bridge.

10.7   Take the Marquette Avenue exit to leave bridge. *Caution:* Sewer grates and glass on exit ramp.

10.9   Stop sign. Turn immediately onto sidewalk bike path to curve right under bridge.

11.1   Veer left as bike path ends and cement sidewalk begins. Railroad tracks immediately after path ends. After railroad tracks, turn right to cross road and then begin riding sidewalk on left.

11.2   Veer left to head toward water. Path then makes a sharp right to follow river.

11.4   Return to bridge overpass and boat-launch area.

---

again. At 1.6 miles, turn right onto one-way South Water, the first road after the bridge. Just before making the turn, look left at the fantastic architecture of the building that houses the Old Bar, on the corner. This section of the ride passes through a quiet old industrial area with wide streets.

Check out the great old watertower to the right, at 2.6 miles, before the left turn onto Cass Avenue. This wide road has old houses and plenty of big trees. At 4.7 miles, it suddenly turns flat with farmland. Cross M–15, where the shoulder becomes wider and newer. Turn left onto the wide shoulder of Pine Street; from here the view runs all the way to the city's spires and watertowers. Another left and ride on the good shoulder of Youngs Ditch Road.

At 7.1 miles, a pedestrian crossing sign shows where to turn right onto the Bay-Hampton Rail-Trail. The rail-trail starts with trees, benches, and flowers on either side. At the trailhead and at each intersection are wooden gates to keep motorized vehicles out. *Go slowly* because the turns weaving between each set of gates are tight. At 8.4 miles, cross busy Center Avenue, where there are restaurants to the right. The rail-trail becomes more picturesque here, with many old-fashioned benches and streetlights.

Just before the end of the rail-trail, turn right onto North Madison Avenue and ride to Woodside Avenue. Cross the street and ride the bike lane. At 10.6 miles, the route goes up and over the river on Liberty Bridge. *Watch* for glass and sewer grates on this section. While you're on the bridge, don't miss seeing the old bridge, to the right.

Take the Marquette Avenue exit off the bridge to a path that curves under the bridge and returns the ride to the riverside. Pass a marina and Liberty Harbor before returning along the riverwalk to the starting point. Ride the riverwalk again for interesting people-watching and another view of the Saginaw River.

Riding the Pere Marquette

Number of miles: 32.3
Approximate pedaling time: 3½ hours
Terrain: Flat and rolling hills
Traffic: Low to moderate
Things to see: A Tridge, Tittabawassee and Chippewa Rivers, Pere Marquette Rail-Trail
Food: Alex's Railside Restaurant, 7.8 miles; village of Sanford; 26.4 miles, grocery store

The Tridge is one of the wonderful parts of this ride, and it's right at the beginning. The Tridge is a three-sectioned "bridge" that crosses the confluence of the Tittabawassee and Chippewa Rivers, taking you to any of the three banks along both rivers. It's located in Chippewa Park (the Farmers Market side) in downtown Midland—a beautiful park with flowers, trees, benches, drinking water, and rest rooms.

The Pere Marquette Rail-Trail begins at the foot of the Tridge. It's a wonderful ride along the Tittabawassee River. At press time, the trail offers a 21-mile ride to Coleman. However, every year the trail seems to grow longer—due to the great work by the Friends of the Pere Marquette Rail-Trail. You'll enjoy 13 miles of the rail-trail before branching off to hit the beautiful country roads. For a great but shorter ride, stick to the trail both ways.

The rail-trail is loaded with signs to make the going easier. At each intersection, signs show where you are as well as the next stop you'll have to make. There are also old cement signposts along the way (like SAG 21, which lets you know you're 21 miles from Saginaw).

Leave Chippewa Park heading northwest for a delightful section

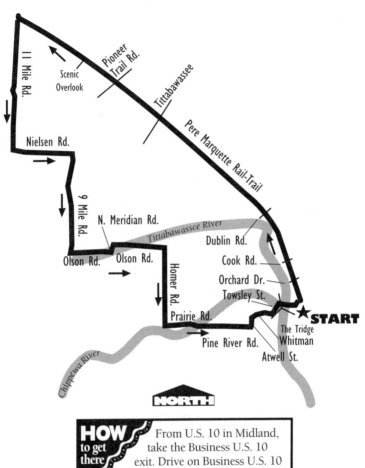

11 Mile Rd.

Pioneer Trail Rd.

Scenic Overlook

Tittabawassee

Pere Marquette Rail-Trail

Nielsen Rd.

9 Mile Rd.

N. Meridian Rd.

Tittabawassee River

Dublin Rd.

Cook Rd.

Olson Rd.   Olson Rd.

Orchard Dr.

Homer Rd.

Towsley St.

★ **START**

Prairie Rd.

The Tridge

Pine River Rd.   Whitman

Atwell St.

Chippewa River

NORTH

HOW to get there
From U.S. 10 in Midland, take the Business U.S. 10 exit. Drive on Business U.S. 10 to Ashman Street. Turn to drive southwest, and Ashman Street dead-ends into a parking lot at the base of the Tridge.

0.0   Look for PERE MARQUETTE RAIL-TRAIL signs from the parking lot at the base of the Tridge.

0.9   Stop at Orchard Drive and continue on rail-trail.

1.5   Stop and cross Cook Road.

2.3   Stop and cross road.

2.9   Stop and cross Dublin Road.

4.7   Stop and cross Tittabawassee.

5.8   Stop and cross Pioneer Trail Road.

5.9   Scenic overlook.

6.6   *Use caution* when crossing driveway; four driveways follow in next 1.2 miles.

8.2   Stop and cross Cedar Street.

8.4   Stop and cross road.

8.6   Stop and cross 7 Mile Road

9.7   Stop and cross 8 Mile Road.

10.8   Stop and cross 9 Mile Road.

12.3   Stop and cross 10½ Mile Road.

13.0   Stop and turn left onto 11 Mile Road.

15.3   Stop and turn left onto Nielsen Road.

17.3   Stop and turn right onto 9 Mile Road.

20.3   At four-way stop, turn left onto Olson Road.

23.4   Stop and turn left onto North Meridian Road.

23.5   Turn right onto Olson Road.

25.4   Stop and turn right onto Homer Road.

26.4   After stoplight at M–20, continue straight.

27.0   Blinking light at Chippewa River Road.

27.4   Take first left after river to turn onto Prairie Road.

28.6   Road becomes Pine River Road.

30.0   After a series of curves, road become Atwell Street.

31.1   Road curves right and becomes Whitman.

32.0   Turn left onto Towsley Street.

32.2   Turn left onto paved path to Tridge.

32.3   Return to the start of Pere Marquette Rail-Trail.

along the Tittabawassee River. After a stop sign, there's Emerson Park on the left, so there's only a park between the rail-trail and the river. Cross a creek, at 1.1 miles, as the Tittabawassee River swings away from the rail-trail. There's still plenty to see. At 1.4 miles, on your left, the Herbert H. Dow Historical Museum takes over—it looks like an old small town. Then, at 2.9 miles, cross Dublin Road.

The rail-trail continues mostly flat and straight. Farther out of downtown Midland, you'll see more and more types of birds, trees, wildflowers, and wild berries. At 5.9 miles, the Averill Rollway overlook, on the left, offers another view of the Tittabawassee River as well as the opportunity to see a historic spot. This is where lumbermen kept logs in the winter before sending them downriver to the Saginaw mills in the spring.

Big trees return just before Alex's Railside Restaurant, at 7.8 miles on the right. At Cedar Street, at 8.2 miles, you can ride to the right to enter the village of Sanford, where snacks and drinks are available.

Just before the stop sign at 8.4 miles, there are bathrooms on the left side of the trail. Continue on for great views from bridges at 8.5 and 8.9 miles. Beautiful scenery continues as the ride crosses 8, 9 and 10½ Mile roads on the way to the stop sign at 11 Mile Road. Turn left and leave the rail-trail behind.

The quiet countryside envelops you on this mostly flat and straight road. Low traffic and old trees make riding pleasant. A few houses cause breaks in the trees on 11 Mile Road, but not on Nielsen Road, which the ride turns onto at 15.3 miles. This, too, is flat and straight riding.

At the first stop sign, the loop turns right onto 9 Mile Road. At 19.2 miles, a small uphill breaks up the mostly flat and straight stretch. After a left turn on Olson Road, pines scent the air. Easy riding on Olson Road continues after a short jog on North Meridian Road, and the scenery changes from trees to houses and fields.

A right turn onto Homer Road at 25.4 miles brings more easy riding on a low-traffic road. After Homer crosses M–20 at 26.4 miles, traffic becomes heavier. Enjoy the peaceful Chippewa River at 27.2 miles before turning onto Prairie Road. At the intersection is a Methodist church and the Homer Cemetery.

By 28.8 miles, the road has become Pine River Road, and the river runs close by. At 29.4 miles, on the left, the Chippewa River Nature Center offers a great place for a break. A series of curves changes the road to Atwell Street and then Whitman. Turn left onto a hard-packed dirt road, Towsley Street, for a short jog to the Tridge. A short, hard uphill brings you to the top of the Tridge. Veer right, ride a short but sweet downhill, and you're back to where you began this picturesque ride.

Saginaw Sashay

Number of miles:	8.9
Approximate pedaling time:	1 hour
Terrain:	Mostly flat
Traffic:	Avoid street riding during rush hour
Things to see:	Saginaw River, Wickes Park, Old Town, Ojibway Island
Food:	Fast food and bar, 2.3 miles; bar and restaurant, 2.7 miles; fast food, 4.5 miles

Never has so much been packed into such a short ride as the Saginaw Sashay, with the possible exception of Mackinac Island—parks, a riverwalk, an island, and Old Town, a section near the river filled with old brick buildings rejuvenated with new and interesting shops.

Pedal off from the southern parking lot of Wickes Park, near the soccer and softball fields. Ride west on Wickes Park Drive, a wide, paved road, and the Saginaw River lies before you. At 0.1 mile, the road curves right and you ride alongside the river. This is all part of Wickes Park, filled with trees, playgrounds, rest rooms, and the quiet river.

At 1.6 miles, the road curves right. To the left is the bike path that you will return on later. There are two left turns, and the route rides over the river and bike path, offering a pleasant view of both. Ride the sidewalk here, as there's not much room on the road, and traffic on Rust Avenue can be heavy.

Leave the traffic behind with a right turn onto South Hamilton Street. This wide, quiet street leads to Old Town. Pass restaurants, bars, stores, and a bicycle shop, at 2.4 miles. A right turn onto West

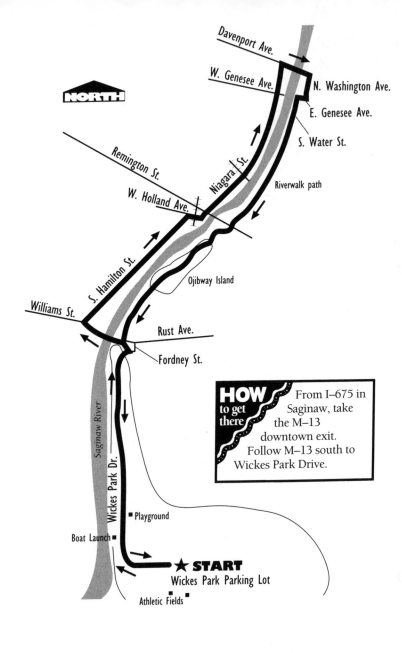

Davenport Ave.

W. Genesee Ave.

N. Washington Ave.

E. Genesee Ave.

S. Water St.

NORTH

Remington St.

Niagara St.

Riverwalk path

W. Holland Ave.

S. Hamilton St.

Ojibway Island

Williams St.

Rust Ave.

Fordney St.

HOW to get there From I–675 in Saginaw, take the M–13 downtown exit. Follow M–13 south to Wickes Park Drive.

Saginaw River

Wickes Park Dr.

■ Playground

Boat Launch ■

★ **START**
Wickes Park Parking Lot

■   ■
Athletic Fields

0.0 From parking area by softball and soccer fields in Wickes Park, ride west on Wickes Park Drive.

0.1 Turnout to left. Follow road as it curves right.

1.6 Again, follow road as it curves right.

1.7 Park road dead-ends. Stop, cross, and turn left onto Fordney Street.

1.8 Turn left onto Rust Avenue at traffic light. Ride sidewalk over bridge; road becomes Williams Street.

2.1 Railroad crossing. Cross Niagara Street.

2.2 Turn right onto South Hamilton Street.

2.3 Enter Old Town area.

2.4 Bicycle shop.

2.6 Continue straight at traffic light.

3.1 Stop and turn right onto West Holland Avenue.

3.2 Move into left lane, cross railroad tracks, and turn left onto Niagara Street. Continue straight after stop at Remington Street. *Caution:* Watch for automobiles turning right onto Niagara Street from bridge.

3.7 Railroad crossing.

4.2 Traffic light at West Genesee Avenue.

4.4 Stop and turn right at Davenport Avenue. Ride sidewalk over bridge.

4.5 Turn right onto North Washington Avenue.

4.6 Turn right at East Genesee Avenue.

4.7 Turn left at South Water Street.

4.8 Riverwalk path begins.

6.1 Veer right onto bridge to park on Ojibway Island. Lake Linton to left.

6.4 Join park road with bike lane.

6.6 Curve left, cross bridge, and curve right onto sidewalk to leave Ojibway Island.

6.8 Follow riverwalk path as it curves right and left to pass under bridge.

7.3   Path ends. Ride up small hill and turn right onto Wickes Park
      Drive.

8.9   Return to Wickes Park parking area.

Holland Avenue, at 3.1 miles, changes the view from Old Town to the
Saginaw River. Move into the left lane to turn left onto Niagara Street.
Cross railroad tracks before swinging left and stopping in the traffic
island to cross Remington Street.

The wide, low-traffic Niagara Street curves right and left before
showing the river. Cross railroad tracks at 3.7 miles; don't miss the
beautiful old railroad bridge over the river. Cross the river via Davenport Avenue. Here again the safest way to travel is the sidewalk, and
curb cuts on both sides make it easy.

Saginaw's Civic Center marks the intersection for the right onto
North Washington Avenue, and a quick peek at downtown. Break off
from the ride here if you're interested in exploring some of the beautiful old buildings Saginaw has to offer. If not, turn right after one
block and you're back to the river. At 4.9 miles, the path begins.
Work your way toward the path through the parking lot or wait for a
cutout in the curb.

Soon the water will be at your toes. Watch for herons flying lazily
down the river. Cross railroad tracks and look right for a good view
of an old railroad bridge. Next, the ride leads to Potthoff Park. At 6.0
miles, the riverwalk winds down and up and left and right to the
bridge to Ojibway Island. The riverwalk becomes a bike lane on the
road around the island. This is a good spot to add mileage to the
route by looping around the island on the wide drive. Lake Linton, to
the east, forms the other watery boundary to the island.

Several curves take you off the island to where the riverwalk path
begins again. If you ride around dusk, keep on eye out for a wood-
chuck that lives in the area, at 6.9 miles. Pass the YMCA just before
curving down and under another traffic bridge. The riverwalk ends at
Wickes Park, at 7.3 miles. Ride up a small hill, turn right, and you're
back on Wickes Park Drive. Another run along the river returns the
ride to the parking lot, at 8.9 miles.

The Clio Creek Circuit

Number of miles: 26.8
Approximate pedaling time: 3½ hours
Terrain: Rolling hills and flat
Traffic: Heavy during rush hour on M–57 and M–54
Things to see: Clio Bike Path, Clio Creek, and Buell Lake
Food: In Otisville, Buell Lake Patio 'n' Pub; Witmer's Grocery, 21.6 miles

The small town of Clio is big on parks and bike paths. Begin this ride at City Park along the banks of Clio Creek. The bike path goes northwest to McCormick Park (a nice, short side trip) and south to the outskirts of town. This route heads south, leaving City Park with Clio Creek on the right. Immediately pass under a bridge—don't miss the mural painted on it. Veer right at 0.3 mile, and continue to veer right each time the path branches left. At 0.4 mile, ride up and over on a bridge and pass a clearing with picnic tables.

The bike path ends at 1.1 miles. Plans have been made to continue the path to create a loop around the county. It will be hard, though, to beat the beauty of this circuit.

Turn left onto Wilson Road and enjoy a small shoulder. Pass the Clio Fireman's Park on the left, at 2.3 miles. Continue on, stopping at North Saginaw (M–54), Lewis, Bray, Center, Genesee, and Irish Roads. This stretch begins flat but later has some rolling hills. Large homes and old barns line the route.

At 9.8 miles, pass Burroughs Lake on the left. Then Wilson Road becomes curvy and lined with pines as it winds its way into Otisville. Stop at downtown Otisville, at 11.5 miles, and turn onto

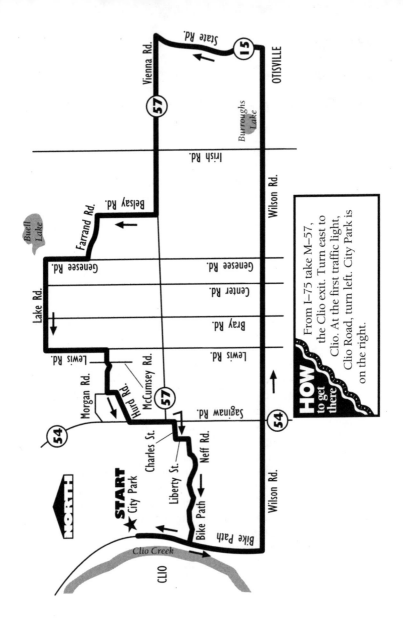

NORTH

Buell Lake

Burroughs Lake

Clio Creek

CLIO

START
★ City Park

HOW to get there

From I–75 take M–57, the Clio exit. Turn east to Clio. At the first traffic light, Clio Road, turn left. City Park is on the right.

State Rd.

Vienna Rd.

Irish Rd.

Farrand Rd.

Belsay Rd.

Genesee Rd.

Genesee Rd.

Lake Rd.

Center Rd.

Bray Rd.

Lewis Rd.

Lewis Rd.

McCumsey Rd.

Morgan Rd.

Hurd Rd.

Saginaw Rd.

Charles St.

Liberty St.

Neff Rd.

Bike Path

Bike Path

Wilson Rd.

Wilson Rd.

OTISVILLE

15

57

57

54

54

0.0 From the southern end of the parking lot in City Park, head south on the bike path, with Clio Creek on your right.

0.3 Veer right to stay on route.

0.4 Veer right to stay on route.

1.1 Bike path ends at gate. Turn left onto Wilson Road.

2.2 Stop and continue straight across North Saginaw Road. (M–54).

3.5 Stop and continue straight across Lewis Road.

4.5 Stop and continue straight across Bray Road.

5.5 Stop and continue straight across Center Road.

6.5 Stop and continue straight across Genesee Road.

9.6 Stop and continue straight across Irish Road.

10.9 Otisville town limits.

11.5 Stop at State Road (M–15) and turn left.

12.6 Turn left onto Vienna Road (M–57).

15.6 Turn right onto Belsay Road.

16.6 Turn left onto Farrand Road.

17.6 Stop and turn right onto Genesee Road.

18.6 Turn left onto Lake Road.

19.6 Stop and continue straight across Center Road.

20.6 Stop and continue straight across Bray Road.

21.6 Turn left at four-way stop at Lewis Road.

23.1 Turn right onto Hurd Road.

23.9 Turn left at stop sign at McCumsey Road. Take immediate curve to right onto Morgan Road.

24.4 Road curves left and right and becomes Hurd Road.

25.1 Stop and turn left onto M–54, Saginaw Road.

25.2 Continue straight across Vienna Road at traffic light.

25.3 Turn right at Charles Street.

25.35 Turn left at Liberty Street.

25.4 Turn right at Neff Road.

25.5 Turn right onto bike path.

25.8 Continue straight as spur on right leads to shopping area.

26.3 Veer right at Y.
26.4 Continue straight as spur on right leads to residential area.
26.7 Blind curve.
26.8 Return to park. Tar path on right leads to parking area.

State Road (M–15). A bike path leads to the edge of town, or you can ride the road.

Turn left onto Vienna Road's (M–57's) wide shoulder, at 12.6 miles. It's busy, but its shoulder makes for safe riding, except during rush hour. This section features several nice ponds and marshes on both sides of the road. Flat becomes rolling hills on Belsay Road. Enjoy a mile of farms and barns before turning left onto Farrand Road.

Farrand Road has a well-kept gravel and dirt surface. The mile of extra pedaling effort is paid off with a cool canopy of green covering the road and the Ligon Outdoor Center, at 16.9 miles.

Get ready for more hills on Genesee Road. If you want a break from the hills take a short side trip to undeveloped Buell Lake. Three locations offer good places for a break: the public access, at 0.1 mile past Lake Road; the park, at 0.2 mile past Lake Road; or the Buell Lake Patio 'n' Pub, at the corner of Genesee and Lake Roads. All you'll hear at the first two places is the splash of fish jumping out of the water. At the third spot, of course, it's the splashing of beverages.

Lake Road begins with a small hill and flattens out before more small hills. At 21.6 miles, a fruit stand and grocery store offer provisions. Turn left here onto Lewis Road. Pass horses and ponds before the right turn onto Hurd Road. At the stop at McCumsey Road, the route jogs left and the road becomes Morgan Road. After more curves, it turns into Hurd Road. At 25.1 miles, stop at Saginaw Road (M–54).

The next stretch is short but heavily traveled. A wide shoulder on Saginaw Road helps, but it disappears at the light with Vienna Road.

The traffic only lasts 0.2 mile, though. With a right turn at Charles Street, quiet roads take you back to the bike path.

The path here is short but wonderful. Begin with a long sweeping downhill that leads to a baby-blue bridge. Bike tires make a great sound over the wood planks. Complete the ride by pedaling around curves, over small creeks, and through large drainage pipes made into tunnels. The path meanders back to the main creek at 26.3 miles, and it leads you back to the park to complete the ride.

The James S. Miner Riverwalk

Number of miles:	14.1
Approximate pedaling time:	2 hours
Terrain:	Mostly flat
Traffic:	Light
Things to see:	Shiawassee River, historic village in McCurdy Park, boyhood home of Thomas E. Dewey, Curwood Castle, towns of Owosso and Corunna
Food:	Grocery store, 4.7 miles; corner store, 8.8 miles; grocery store, 12.1 miles; fast food, 12.4 miles; stores in Corunna, 13.5 miles

The James S. Miner Riverwalk offers a wonderful combination—an unspoiled, peaceful, tree-filled section that winds along with the Shiawassee River, and a section that leads to many of the area's historical attractions. And all this in only 5 miles. The rest of the loop twists and turns through old residential sections and farmlands before returning to the banks of the Shiawassee River.

Begin in Corunna's McCurdy Park. Before or after the ride, bike to the southwest corner of the park to visit the Shiawassee Valley Historic Village, where several historic buildings have been moved here to form a village: the 1888 Christ Evangelical Church, with stained-glass windows and pipe organ, where you may see a wedding in progress; the Lemon School, sparkling white with black shutters, and, of course, a school bell; and other buildings still under restoration. The park also offers tree-shaded picnic tables, drinking water, and rest rooms.

Wilkinson Rd.

52

Shiawassee River

Green Meadows Park

Path

N. Shiawassee

Hickory Rd.

Copas Rd.

State Rd.

North St.

Dewey

Gould St.

King St.

Copas Rd.

Pine St.

Oliver St.

Williams St.

OWOSSO

Curwood Castle

Comstock Cabin

Jerome St.

Oak St.

Oakwood

Rawleigh St.

Grover St.

Path

21

Lion's Park

S. Washington St.

CORUNNA

McCurdy Park

START ★

Norton St.

Heritage Park

Shiawassee County Courthouse

71

Corunna Ave.

HOW to get there From I–69 take exit 105 and drive north on M–52 to Owosso. In Owosso, turn right onto Main Street (M–21). Then turn right onto Water Street, following the signs for M–71. From Water Street, turn right onto South Washington Street and left onto Corunna Avenue (M–71). Drive southeast on M–71 toward the town of Corunna. Just before downtown Corunna, drive past the park to turn left onto Norton Street, which dead-ends in McCurdy Park.

0.0 From McCurdy Park, ride to the pedestrian bridge. Ride the bridge over the river. After crossing, make an immediate left to follow path.

1.6 Veer right to stay on path; path becomes paved.

1.7 Curve left; path joins Grover Street. Continue straight.

2.0 Curve right onto Rawleigh Street. In mid-curve, veer left, where unpaved path resumes.

2.3 Continue straight as another branch of path veers right.

2.5 Path dead-ends into cross street, Oakwood (no sign). Turn right.

2.6 Turn left onto Jerome Street, first street on left.

2.9 Stop and continue straight past Oak Street.

3.0 Lion's Park.

3.2 Stop and cross South Washington Street before turning left and path begins on right just before the bridge.

3.3 Path becomes paved.

3.4 Veer left under bridge.

3.6 Continue straight as another path veers left.

3.7 Stop and continue straight across Williams Street.

3.8 Turn left onto Oliver Street without crossing street.

3.85 Boyhood home of Thomas E. Dewey on left.

3.86 Turn right onto Pine Street, crossing Oliver Street.

4.0 Stop and cross King Street before turning left.

4.1 Stop and cross North Shiawassee (M–52), before turning right and riding sidewalk bike route.

4.7 Veer left onto wide asphalt path away from sidewalk, just before grocery store.

4.9 Veer left onto road and follow road as it curves right alongside river.

5.1 Continue straight as pavement ends.

5.2 Turn left onto paved road.

5.3 Enter Green Meadows Park. Continue straight past gate as pavement ends and dirt path begins.

5.6	Cross creek on bridge.
5.8	Turn right to ride up steep hill with rain gullies to spot where Wilkinson Road dead-ends.
5.9	Continue straight on Wilkinson Road.
6.3	Stop and continue straight across M–52.
6.8	At dead-end, turn right onto Hickory Road.
7.8	Continue straight after four-way stop with North Street.
8.3	Jog left after four-way stop with King Street to continue on Hickory Road.
8.4	Stop and then turn left onto Oliver Street.
8.7	Continue straight after four-way stop at Dewey.
9.0	Continue straight after four-way stop with Gould Street.
9.4	Curve left, road becomes Copas Road.
11.4	Stop and turn right onto State Road.
12.4	Continue straight at traffic light with M–21. (Cross State Road to ride paved bike path.)
12.9	Bike path begins on west side of State Road.
13.5	Ride bridge across river.
13.6	Turn right onto Corunna Avenue (M–71).
13.9	Turn right onto Norton Street, into McCurdy Park.
14.1	Road ends in parking lot of McCurdy Park.

Move back along the river and cross the footbridge, where ducks lazily drift with the current and float by. Make a sharp left and enter a dark, green tunnel made by trees and ferns, with glimpses of the glistening Shiawassee River on the left. This part of the path is fast going but unpaved, and it can be muddy in spots just after a rain.

The path enters a residential section at 1.6 miles, when it veers right and becomes paved. At 2.0 miles, the river appears again as the road curves right and becomes Rawleigh Street. Veer left at mid-curve here, and follow the river once again. Take to the streets when the path dead-ends next to the Oakwood Street Footbridge. Turn right and left to pass Lion's Park, a favorite with ducks and geese.

A short ride after crossing South Washington Street brings you to the wide, paved section of the path. Flowering crabtrees line the river and explode with blossoms in the spring. At 3.6 miles, pass the huge fieldstone pillars of the Heritage Footbridge. Across the river you can see the Comstock Cabin—Owosso's oldest building—built in 1836, and the huge Curwood Castle, the former home of James Oliver Curwood, an author and photographer in the early 1900s.

Continue past the old-fashioned streetlights and benches along the river and ride up a small slope to Williams Street. Twisting and turning through a residential area, the route next passes the boyhood home of Thomas E. Dewey, former governor of New York and presidential candidate in 1944 and 1948.

Cross M–52 to the bike route on the sidewalk. Veer left at 4.9 miles, cruising through several downhill curves to regain the river in Green Meadows Park. The park features picnic tables and portable toilets. Here the path becomes dirt again as you continue along the banks of the Shiawassee River amidst hardwoods.

At 5.8 miles, encounter the biggest challenge: a short, steep hill rutted from rain runoff. To be perfectly honest, a mountain bike probably couldn't do this hill. But it was the only way to include as much of the beautiful river as possible. And it's only a few yards. At the top, a fast, flat, paved section begins through the wide streets of Owosso neighborhoods. Wind through the residential area past fine old homes to the city limits, at 9.0 miles. Farms, fields, and wildflowers dominate until businesses begin again, at 12.4 miles. It's a great section through the countryside.

Less than a mile later, the Shiawassee River appears again. Heritage Park, 13.3 miles, offers a great spot to enjoy the river and a small falls. Cross the river and move into downtown Corunna, with the Shiawassee County Courthouse at 13.6 miles. Turn right here, returning to McCurdy Park.

34 A Capital Ride on the Lansing River Trail

Number of miles:	9.9
Approximate pedaling time:	1 hour
Terrain:	Mostly flat
Traffic:	Light
Things to see:	Grand and Red Cedar Rivers, Potter Park/Zoo, Capitol Building, Turner/Dodge House, Brenke Fish Ladder
Food:	Best Steak House #16 and Speedway, 5.2 miles; many restaurants along Michigan Avenue

Incredible. Fantastic. Not enough can be said about what the people of Lansing, Michigan's state capital, have done in creating the river trail. They reclaimed a stretch of land along the east side of the Grand River (the northern two-thirds of the trail) and the Red Cedar River (the southern third) and transformed it into a quiet oasis in the middle of the noisy city.

Varying between sections of wide wood planks and smooth asphalt, the tree-lined river trail is dotted with scenic overlooks, historic landmarks, and other points of interest. You'll share the trail with swooping swallows and frolicking squirrels.

This ride starts from a northern point on the river trail and rides southeast to the trail's end. From there, the brave face Lansing street traffic and are rewarded with a tour of downtown and a circle around the restored Capitol Building. For the faint of heart or those with children, there's the option of retracing your steps on the river trail—it's well worth a repeat performance.

Begin at the Turner/Dodge House, built in the 1850s by James

Turner, an early Lansing pioneer and entrepreneur. From owning a general store, he became involved with government, serving the state as deputy treasure and state senator. The house, high atop a bank of the Grand River, was later purchased by Frank L. Dodge, Turner's son-in-law. In 1974 the city bought the house and surrounding property to make a park.

From the Turner/Dodge House, you're just a curve away from the tree-lined trail, which has quarter-mile markers, rest rooms, and drinking fountains along the way. The first stop, just south of the house, is the North Lansing Dam and Brenke Fish Ladder, the sixth in a series to help salmon and trout make their way from Lake Michigan to South Lansing Dam—a trip of 184 miles. The park around the fish ladder has picnic tables and rest rooms.

Continuing on the river trail, the river flows on the right, and trees on the left block the sounds of downtown traffic. Gentle curves and small hills keep the terrain interesting. In the late afternoon, when the trail gets busy, *take care* around the curves—in-line skaters wearing headphones often can't hear you coming.

After 3 miles, the river trail winds its way into the Potter Park/Zoo. Make sure to give the ducks and geese the right-of-way as they waddle from pond to pond. James Potter donated the land to the city for the park, and it was later filled by donations of elk from James Moore and raccoons from Charles Davis. It's a great place for a break, with picnic tables, drinking water, and rest rooms.

With more curves and gentle rises and falls, the river trail dead-ends at a parking lot on Clippert Street. Ride that wide road north to Michigan Avenue, the tricky part of the ride. With many lanes feeding into the intersection, *use caution* when crossing Michigan. Turning left, west, onto Michigan Avenue, ride the sidewalk for the first .25 mile. The road then widens, and you can swing down into the street to ride. Shortly after braving the Michigan Avenue crossing, you're rewarded by a fantastic view of the Capitol Building, as Michigan Avenue heads straight into it and dead-ends there. Circle the restored building, or stop for a tour of it, and then ride north through a quiet residential area to rejoin the trail for a hill up to the Turner/Dodge House.

★ START
Turner/Dodge House

NORTH

Seymour St.

River Trail

Ionia St.

Walnut St.

Capital Ave.

Capitol
Building

Washtenaw St.

Michigan Ave.

Clippert St.

Spring St.

River Trail

Potter
Park/Zoo

Red Cedar River

Grand River

HOW to get there From I–496 in Lansing, take Cedar Street/ Larch Street, exit 7. Drive north on Larch Street to Grand River Avenue. Turn left and right onto Turner Street. Turn left onto River Drive (look for the bicycle path sign). The road curves to the right. Park on the left at the Turner/Dodge House.

DIREC-TIONS at a glance

0.0 From the parking lot of the Turner/Dodge House, head south on river trail. Follow RIVER TRAIL signs.

2.1 River trail runs into Spring Street. A quick jog to the right and you're back on the trail.

2.3 River trail bears right.

3.1 River trail enters Potter Park/Zoo.

3.3 Stop sign at zoo admission gate.

5.1 Trail ends at parking lot, the dead end of Clippert Street. Turn left onto Clippert Street.

5.2 Stop and cross Kalamazoo Street.

5.5 Turn left onto Michigan Avenue.

7.3 Cross railroad tracks.

7.9 From the right-hand lane, turn left onto one-way Capital Avenue.

8.0 Turn right onto Washtenaw Street.

8.2 Turn right onto Walnut Street. Move into center lane to continue straight.

8.5 Turn right onto Ionia Street. Move into left lane.

8.6 Turn left onto Seymour Street.

8.65 Stop and continue straight across Shiawassee Street.

9.0 Continue straight after stop sign at Saginaw Street.

9.1 Stop and continue straight across Madison Street.

9.2 Continue straight after stop sign at Oakland Avenue.

9.4 Continue straight after four-way stop. Seymour Street becomes Grand River Avenue.

9.5 Traffic light.

9.6 Sharp right just after bridge to return to the trail. Bear left onto trail.

9.9 Turner/Dodge House and parking lot on left.

Jackson's Portage Lake Loop

Number of miles:	30.6
Approximate pedaling time:	4 hours
Terrain:	Rolling hills
Traffic:	Moderate
Things to see:	Portage Lake, Waterloo Recreation Area, Jackson County Park, wide range of scenery
Food:	Country stores at 12.4 miles and 13.5 miles

Some of the prettiest country roads in Michigan are on this ride. If you don't like one stretch, just keep pedaling, and something different will soon appear around one of the many curves. The terrain varies from flat to rolling hills to flat again, offering variety every other mile or so. At the sides of the road, you'll find marshes, creeks, ponds, and lakes. There's also a lovely mixture of evergreens and deciduous trees.

Two nice places for picnics or breaks are the Portage Lake Unit of the Waterloo Recreation Area, on the southwest side of Big Portage Lake, and the Jackson County Park, on the east side of the lake.

Get ready for the ride at the William J. Nixon Memorial Park. Head east on North Street, a wide residential road with trees. Elm Street offers the same. Make sure to bypass Blakley Road, at 1.1 miles. The route soon turns right onto Blake Road, at 1.8 miles. Blake Road runs along the expressway as it winds toward Dettman Road. Cross over the expressway on Dettman Road and say good-bye to traffic and noise as you ride its wide shoulder.

Turn right at the great tree at Seymour Avenue, and ride the small

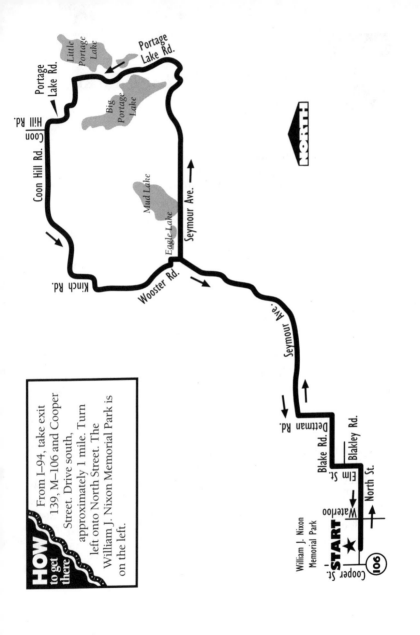

HOW to get there

From I-94, take exit 139, M-106 and Cooper Street. Drive south, approximately 1 mile. Turn left onto North Street. The William J. Nixon Memorial Park is on the left.

NORTH

Little Portage Lake

Portage Lake Rd.

Portage Lake Rd.

Coon Hill Rd.

Coon Hill Rd.

Big Portage Lake

Mud Lake

Eagle Lake

Seymour Ave.

Kinch Rd.

Wooster Rd.

Seymour Ave.

Dettman Rd.

Blake Rd.

Blakley Rd.

Elm St.

Waterloo

North St.

William J. Nixon Memorial Park

START

106

Cooper St.

DIRECTIONS at a glance

0.0	From William J. Nixon Memorial Park parking lot, turn left onto North Street.
0.3	Traffic light at Waterloo.
0.9	Stop and turn left onto Elm Street.
1.1	Do *not* turn onto Blakley Road.
1.8	Turn right onto Blake Road.
2.8	Stop and turn left onto Dettman Road.
3.3	Stop and turn right onto Seymour Avenue.
6.3	Hard right then left (straight is Sargent Road).
7.0	Hard left (to right is Smith Road).
7.5	Hard right (left is St. John's).
8.1	Hard right (to left is Wooster Road).
12.4	Turn left onto Portage Lake Road.
14.7	Curve left (Huttenlocker is straight).
16.2	Stop and continue straight onto Coon Hill Road.
19.4	Curve left (Kinch Road to right).
19.9	Curve right (Krofft to left).
20.2	Turn left onto Wooster Road.
21.1	Curve left (Root Station Road to right).
22.5	Stop and turn right onto Seymour Avenue.
27.3	Turn left onto Dettman Road.
27.8	Turn right onto Blake Road.
28.8	Stop and turn left onto Elm Street.
29.7	Turn right onto North Street.
30.3	Traffic light at Waterloo.
30.6	Turn right into parking lot of William J. Nixon Memorial Park.

shoulder east over rolling hills, past farms and trees. There's not much traffic here, and what there is moves at low speeds. After the cemetery, at 4.8 miles, two curves left lead to a marshy area on the right. As promised, the hills give way to flatter terrain, at 5.4 miles. Not much later is a wonderful downhill.

Curves continue at 6.0 miles. There are tight corners at 7.0, 7.5, and 8.1 miles. Less than half a mile later, tall trees shade the road, but after 9.0 miles, you can see a lake through the trees on the left. The trees give way to a marsh on the left, at 10.5 miles, before the big trees return.

At 11.4 miles, the Portage Lake Unit of the Waterloo Recreation Area is on the left. Turn left here and follow the state park road for drinking water, rest rooms, picnic tables, beach access, and great views of the lake through the . . . yes, trees.

Seymour Avenue has a great downhill at 12.0 miles, and the road opens up just before the turn onto Portage Lake Road. Start here with an uphill. Another open stretch announces the arrival of Jackson County Park, also on Big Portage Lake. A break from the rolling hills and curves soon follows, at 13.9 miles. Then a creek, 0.4 mile later, signals more curves and marshes to come.

At 16.2 miles, stop and continue straight on Coon Hill Road. After a hard left at 17.9 miles, there's a breather from hills for 0.7 mile. More curves and hills lead to a left turn onto Wooster Road. The road winds its way to a creek, at 21.7 miles, before the stop at Seymour Avenue, at 22.5 miles. Turn right and ride back on Seymour Avenue for more great scenery from a different perspective than your ride out. Leave the country behind at 27.3 miles with a turn onto Dettman Road. A short jaunt through a residential area returns you to William J. Nixon Memorial Park.

The LakeLands Trail Loop

Number of miles:	27.6 (10 or 15 for shorter loops)
Approximate pedaling time:	4 hours
Terrain:	First half is flat, second has rolling hills
Traffic:	Avoid M–36 at rush hour
Things to see:	Creeks, marshes, birds, wildflowers, Stockbridge's historic village square
Food:	In Gregory, Stockbridge, and Pinckney

LakeLands Trail State Park officially opened in 1994. So far, of the planned 36 miles, 12.6 miles of the crushed-stone trail have been completed. What exists already is fantastic. Because the railroad corridor was abandoned approximately twenty years ago, the vegetation has had years to grow, so you'll find tunnels of trees and in them birds of all colors.

Most of the way is fast going, but there are some piles of gravel around the edges of the trail. Bikes have the right side of the trail, horses the left. It's also well marked for road crossings and driveways. A trail pass may be purchased for a small fee at the Village Cyclery on East Main in Pinckney, before you hit the trail.

Leaving the old depot in Pinckney, heading west, the only sounds on the route comes from crickets and birds living in the marsh on your right. At 1.4 miles, ride a bridge over the creek that winds along with the path. There are bridges again at 1.8, 2.0, and 2.5 miles. Wildflowers and trees offer a nice view before you reach a marsh with an array of plants, flowers, and birds. At 2.8 miles, fields take over.

After the stop for Kelly Road, at 3.1 miles, there's a pond in the field, with horses on the right. The left side of the trail is dominated by a high fence for the University of Michigan's Edwin S. George Bio-

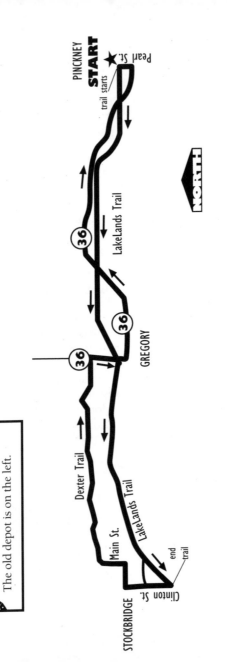

HOW to get there: From U.S. 23, take the M–36 exit and drive west to Pinckney. In Pinckney, turn right onto Pearl Street (D–19). The old depot is on the left.

NORTH

PINCKNEY
START
★ Pearl St.
trail starts

LakeLands Trail

36

36

GREGORY

Dexter Trail

LakeLands Trail

Main St.

Clinton St.

STOCKBRIDGE

end trail

0.0	Leave the old depot parking lot and pick up the LakeLands Trail on the west end.
1.0	Stop and cross M–36.
1.1	Stop and cross Cedar Lake Road.
3.1	Stop and cross Kelly Road.
3.8	Cross driveway.
4.7	Stop and cross M–36. (*Option:* 10-mile loop turns east on M–36 and returns to Pinckney on M–36.)
6.0	Stop and cross Arnold Road.
7.1	Stop and cross Bullis Road.
7.4	Stop and cross M–36. (*Option:* 15-mile loop turns east on M–36 and returns to Pinckney on M–36.)
8.4	Stop and cross VanSyckle Road.
9.1	Stop and cross Dutton Road.
11.5	Stop and cross Brogan Road.
11.7	Stop and cross M–106.
12.2	Stop and cross Williams Road.
12.6	Enter Clinton park-and-ride lot at end of trail. Turn right out of park and ride into Stockbridge.
13.0	At four-way stop, ride straight on Clinton Street, which later becomes Main Street.
14.3	Stop and turn right on Dexter Trail
15.1	At four-way stop with Brogan Road, continue straight.
19.0	Stop and turn right on M–36, Gregory Road.
19.5	Turn left to continue on M–36. *Watch* for oncoming traffic.
27.4	Turn left onto Pearl Street (D–19).
13.0	Turn left into parking lot at old depot.

10 miles or 15 miles

When the trail crosses M–36 at either 4.7 miles or 7.4 miles, head east and follow directions for longer loop to return to old depot in Pinckney.

logical Research Station. At 4.0 miles, the trail crosses the creek again. At 4.7 miles, the trail crosses M–36, and the shorter 10-mile ride turns east to return to Pinckney. On a hot sunny day, 5.0 miles and 5.8 miles are the perfect places to be, as tall trees engulf the trail, and it feels like you are in a cool forest.

At 7.3 miles, the trail passes behind the stores of Gregory. Crossing M–36, 0.1 mile later, turn left and ride into town if you need supplies. You can also turn onto M–36 here and ride it back to Pinckney for a 15-mile ride. The most beautiful stretch of the trail comes next, with a tree canopy, marsh, and pond. For the next 3 miles, the trail passes mostly through tall trees. Then, at 11.5 miles, the trail curves and begins the entry into Stockbridge. It ends at a park-and-ride lot.

For the return trip, turn right out of the lot toward Stockbridge's main street. Ride past the village square, with its park and township offices. These offices are housed in an 1892 building listed on the National Register of Historic Places.

At the four-way stop with M-106, continue straight for a wonderful section through the countryside. On the way out of town on the flat, wide Clinton Street, don't miss the water tower at 13.1 miles. The trees begin less than a mile later. After a sharp right and left turn, Clinton Street becomes Main Street. At 14.3 miles, stop and turn right onto Dexter Trail, a low-traffic road filled with farms, cows, fields, and rolling hills. Don't miss one of the best barns at 16.2 miles.

After the four-way stop at Brogan Road, the hills continue. Most of them are long and gentle. The hills wind through a great tunnel of trees at 17.2 miles. Next up are a marsh and a creek as you pedal uphill and curve right to the stop sign with M–36, Gregory Road. Ride a wide shoulder into the town of Gregory, where you'll turn left to continue on M–36.

After Gregory, the curves and trees give way to farms and fields. Along this mostly flat stretch are some wonderful old barns. Pinckney appears by 26 miles. Coming into town there's a cemetery on the right. Curve left, and then you're in downtown Pinckney. A turn left onto Pearl Street (D–19) leads to the old depot at the beginning of the trail.

To Hell and Back

Number of miles:	34.8 (22.0 for shorter loop)
Approximate pedaling time:	4 hours
Terrain:	Rolling hills
Traffic:	Avoid riding during rush hour
Things to see:	Downtown Hell, towns of Dexter and Chelsea, lakes, old barns
Food:	Dam Site Inn, Hell Creek Party Store, and Devil's Den in Hell; country store, 12.2 miles; restaurants and stores in Chelsea and Dexter; country store, 24.9 miles; country store, 29.2 miles

They've heard it all, the people who live in Hell. Some call and ask how hot it is. Some call to find out when Hell freezes over. One couple came to Hell to get married on April Fool's Day. And yes, the road to Hell is paved.

It's not easy finding Hell because people keep stealing the road signs. This "Hellish" business supposedly began in 1850, when a businessman wanted to name the town after himself. The townspeople didn't like the idea, so he told them where to go; he also suggested that they could name the town that, too. And they did.

The ride is any thing *but* hell, with rolling hills, lakes, trees, farms, and the unique towns of Dexter and Chelsea. Begin in downtown Hell: all of three businesses. Stop to buy a bat from Hell at the Devil's Den, snacks from the Hell Creek Party Store, or a meal at Dam Site Inn. For those who don't wish to patronize a business and then use its parking lot while riding, there's an alternate starting point, at the Hudson Mills Metropark.

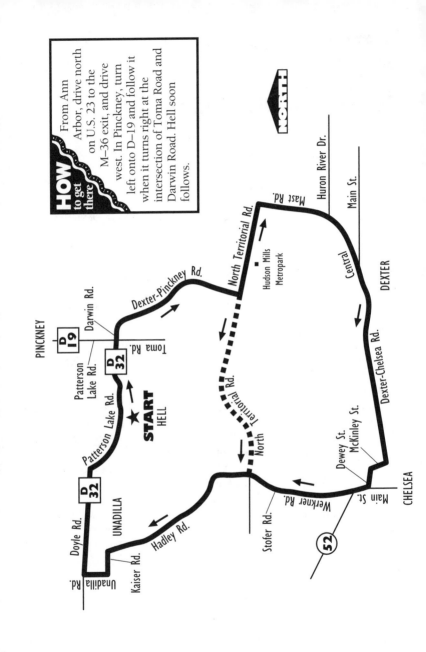

HOW to get there

From Ann Arbor, drive north on U.S. 23 to the M-36 exit, and drive west. In Pinckney, turn left onto D-19 and follow it when it turns right at the intersection of Toma Road and Darwin Road. Hell soon follows.

NORTH

PINCKNEY

D19

D32

Darwin Rd.

Toma Rd.

Patterson Lake Rd.

Patterson Lake Rd.

START

HELL

D32

UNADILLA

Doyle Rd.

Unadilla Rd.

Kaiser Rd.

Hadley Rd.

Dexter-Pinckney Rd.

North Territorial Rd.

Mast Rd.

Huron River Dr.

Main St.

Central

DEXTER

Hudson Mills Metropark

North Territorial Rd.

Stofer Rd.

Werkner Rd.

Dexter-Chelsea Rd.

Dewey St.

McKinley St.

Main St.

CHELSEA

52

0.0 From Hell, ride east on Patterson Lake Road (D–32).

2.2 Continue straight. Road becomes Darwin Road. (Patterson Lake Road is on your left and Toma Road on the right.)

2.7 Stop and turn right onto Dexter-Pinckney Road.

6.9 Turn left onto North Territorial Road at the traffic light. (*Option:* Shorter loop turns right.)

7.3 Hudson Mills Metropark on right. (*Option:* Alternate starting point.)

9.1 Turn right onto Mast Road at blinking light.

12.2 Mast Road becomes Central at Huron River Drive as you enter Dexter.

12.3 Railroad crossing.

12.7 Stop and merge left into traffic onto Main Street.

12.8 Traffic light.

12.9 Turn left onto Dexter-Chelsea Road.

17.2 Two sets of railroad tracks at curve.

19.1 Chelsea village limit.

19.9 Stop and turn right onto McKinley Street.

20.0 Three-way stop, then turn left onto Dewey Street.

20.2 Turn right onto Main Street (M–52).

21.3 Turn right onto Werkner Road (becomes Stofer Road).

24.9 Stop and cross North Territorial Road. Stofer Road becomes Hadley Road.

28.8 Village of Unadilla.

29.1 Stop and turn left onto Kaiser Road. Road quickly curves right and into Unadilla.

30.4 Stop and turn right onto Doyle Road (D–32).

32.6 Road curves right and becomes Patterson Lake Road (also known here as D–32).

34.8 Return to Hell.

22.0 miles

Follow longer loop to intersection of Dexter-Pinckney and North Territorial Roads.

6.9 Turn right onto North Territorial Road.

12.1 Turn right onto Stofer/Hadley Road. Follow longer loop from mile 24.9 back to Hell.

Leaving Hell, the roadside is first lined with trees. It changes to fields and houses about a mile later. This road and the next, Dexter-Pinckney Road, have narrow shoulders, but the speed limit is low. Also, motorists are familiar with bikers using this route. After a series of curves, lakes appear along both sides of Dexter-Pinckney Road. Then it's more trees and curves.

At 6.9 miles, a left turn brings the route to North Territorial Road. It's wide, but it can be very busy at rush hour. The shorter loop turns right here. For the longer loop, the Hudson Mills Metropark is at 7.3 miles, offering drinking water, rest rooms, and a beautiful place for a break.

The trees along the rolling hills give way to farms and fields on Mast Road. Then it's downtown Dexter—another nice spot for a break. Leaving town, the route crosses a bridge and turns left onto Dexter-Chelsea Road. This too has a narrow shoulder. After some picturesque old barns, curves, and a produce stand, at 15.9 miles, it's into the village of Chelsea. At McKinley Street, look straight for a view of the clock tower.

Out of Chelsea, enjoy a wide shoulder on busy M–52 before veering off on Werkner Road. Rolling hills, curves, trees, and old barns again fill the route. Come into the area known as Unadilla, at 28.8 miles, where you'll find a country store. There's another one at 29.2 miles.

Doyle and then Patterson Lake Roads (both designated D–32) offer more nice old barns and trees. The scenery even gets better for a wonderful finish to the ride: By 33.4 miles, treetops throw shadows over the road, followed by a lake on the left, before crossing Hell Creek and riding up the hill into Hell.

38 One Half of A2:
With a Short Cruise Down Easy Street

Number of miles: 27.5 (19.7 for shorter loop)
Approximate pedaling time: 4 hours
Terrain: Rolling hills
Traffic: Avoid all roads at rush hour
Things to see: Scenic Huron River, Gallup Park, old barns, Delphi Metropark
Food: Fast food, 5.4 miles; grocery store, 7.5 miles; shopping mall, 7.9 miles; fast food, 14.4 miles; fast food, 14.8 miles; restaurants on Depot Street, Gallup Park

This ride loops around the western half of Ann Arbor, affectionately known as "A Two" or "A Squared," encompassing several parks, residential and rural areas, hills and flats, and a beautiful home stretch along the Huron River.

Home of the University of Michigan, Ann Arbor has been called the "Athens on the Huron" since the 1800s, for its richness in culture and education. It's also heaven for cyclists, with its many bike paths, lanes, and trails. Between students looking for low-cost transportation and ecology-minded inhabitants, bicycles are everywhere, and drivers are generally biker-friendly.

The ride begins at Gallup Park, a gem along the Huron River. The park has food, drinking water, rest rooms, and a playground, as well as canoe, paddleboat, and bike rentals. At the bottom of the one-lane bridge, you'll find the path where the ride starts. Head directly south, crossing railroad tracks and riding up a small hump before veering left to pick up the bike path. Cross a street, and ride through trees; here the path becomes a bike route through a quiet residential area

filled with elegant homes, beautifully landscaped.

After winding through this area, the route moves across Washtenaw Avenue through another residential area, including Easy Street, at 2.4 miles. Soon it changes to a bike route on the sidewalk along Packard Street. Before you know it you've left Ann Arbor behind and are riding on wide roads with light traffic and little development. Farms, fields, and barns begin in earnest along Scio Church and Zeeb Roads. At 12.4 miles, there's a great treetop view.

At the intersection of Oak Valley Drive and Scio Church Road, the shorter loop turns right, breaking away from the longer loop. The shorter option misses some great countryside riding, but it includes the wonderful ride along the Huron River.

For the shorter ride, the right turn onto Scio Church Road leads to Maple Road. Maple Road winds through a quiet residential section, then a business section (with a sidewalk bike path), before changing again to a rural area. At 13.3 miles, Maple Road ends at Huron River Drive, and the shorter loop joins the longer loop.

Back on the longer ride, pass through the busy intersection of Zeeb and Jackson Roads, at 14.4 miles, just before crossing over I–94. There are several fast-food restaurants here. Just 2.4 miles later, the wonderful barns are traded for a beautiful river. A right turn brings the route onto winding Huron River Drive, a favorite with Ann Arbor cyclists for its low speed limit, tree canopies, and river views.

Stop and enjoy the river at Delphi Metropark, at 18.8 miles. Located on the river, the metropark offers canoe rentals, drinking water, picnic tables, and rest rooms. More hills and curves lead to the river crossing, at 19.6 miles. Begin a pleasant section of the ride 0.8 mile later, where the river follows the road closely and the trees are especially full.

More nice places to stop, and a way to extend the almost completed section of Huron River Drive, are at Bird Hills Nature Center and Barton Park, at 22.6 miles, and the Barton Park and Oxbow Nature Study Area, at 23.6 miles.

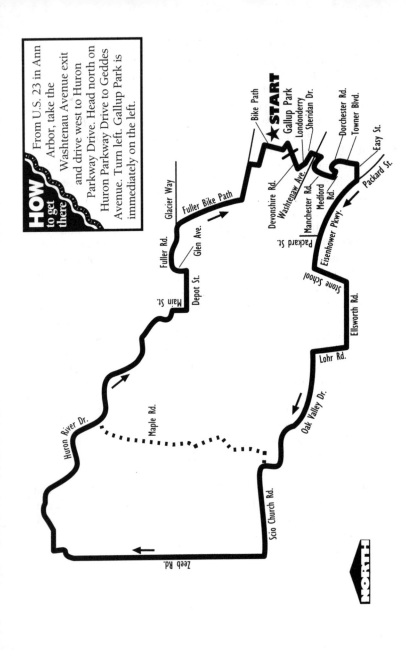

HOW to get there

From U.S. 23 in Ann Arbor, take the Washtenau Avenue exit and drive west to Huron Parkway Drive. Head north on Huron Parkway Drive to Geddes Avenue. Turn left. Gallup Park is immediately on the left.

★ START
Gallup Park
Bike Path

Londonderry
Sheridan Dr.
Dorchester Rd.
Towner Blvd.
Easy St.

Devonshire Rd.
Washtenaw Ave.
Manchester Rd.
Medford Rd.
Packard St.

Packard St.
Eisenhower Pkwy.
Stone School

Fuller Bike Path
Glacier Way
Fuller Rd.
Glen Ave.
Depot St.
Main St.

Huron River Dr.
Maple Rd.
Scio Church Rd.
Zeeb Rd.

Oak Valley Dr.
Lohr Rd.
Ellsworth Rd.

NORTH

DIREC-TIONS
at a glance

0.0 From Gallup Park parking lot at the bottom of the one-lane bridge, head south and immediately cross railroad tracks. Veer left at top of hill. Cross street and follow path as it veers right.

0.1 Veer right as bike path becomes bike route on Devonshire Road.

0.2 Continue straight after three-way stop at Devonshire Road and Spruce.

0.5 Continue straight after all-way stop.

0.8 Turn left onto Londonderry after four-way stop on Devonshire Road.

1.3 Turn left onto Sheridan Drive.

1.5 Continue straight after four-way stop at Bedford.

1.7 Continue straight after traffic light at Washtenaw Avenue. Road becomes Manchester Road. Follow road, not bicycle path signs.

1.8 Turn left to follow Manchester Road. Road curves right then left.

1.9 Turn left at four-way stop with Medford Road.

2.2 Stop and turn left onto Dorchester Road.

2.25 After hard right curve, road becomes Towner Boulevard.

2.4 Stop and turn right onto Easy Street.

2.8 Stop and turn right onto Packard Street. Follow bike route on sidewalk.

3.0 Cobblestone Farm Center and Buhr Park. Rose Park.

3.2 At Y, stop at crosswalk light to cross Packard Street and ride Eisenhower Parkway.

3.4 Turn left onto Stone School.

4.4 Turn right onto Ellsworth Road.

4.8 Traffic light at Varsity Drive.

4.9 Railroad crossing.

5.4 Traffic light at State Street.

6.5 Turn right onto Lohr Road.

7.0 Turn left onto Oak Valley Drive.

7.6	Continue straight after traffic light with Ann Arbor–Saline Road.
7.9	Continue straight after four-way stop with Waters Road.
9.0	Turn left onto Scio Church Road.
10.1	Continue straight after four-way stop at Wagner Road.
12.1	Turn right onto Zeeb Road at four-way stop.
13.1	Continue straight after four-way stop at Liberty Road.
14.4	Continue straight after traffic light at Jackson Road.
14.7	Continue straight after traffic light at freeway exit ramp.
15.7	Continue straight after four-way stop at Dexter–Ann Arbor Road.
16.9	Railroad crossing.
17.0	Stop and turn right onto Huron River Drive.
20.0	Railroad crossing.
22.6	Bird Hills Nature Center and Barton Park.
23.6	Barton Park and Oxbow Nature Study Area.
23.8	Stop and turn right onto Main Street.
24.6	Turn left onto Depot Street.
24.8	Stop and continue straight.
25.2	At traffic light with Glen Avenue, cross street and turn left, riding the sidewalk. Becomes Fuller Road.
25.4	At traffic light, sidewalk becomes bike path.
25.9	Traffic light with Fuller Court. Cross street for bike path. Continue straight until Fuller Road veers right.
26.9	Furstenberg Park Nature Area.
27.2	Turn right into Gallup Park via bike path entrance, crossing Fuller.
27.3	Cross park road.
27.4	Ride across one-lane wooden bridge.
27.5	Return to Gallup Park parking lot.

19.7 miles

Follow longer loop to Scio Church Road.

| 9.0 | Turn right onto Scio Church Road. |
| 9.5 | Turn left at three-way stop onto Maple Road. |

10.4   Continue straight after traffic light at Liberty Road.
10.8   Stop and turn left to continue on Maple Road. (Stadium Boulevard to right.) Bike path on sidewalk.
13.3   Stop and turn right onto Huron River Drive. Follow longer loop directions to return to park at 19.7 miles.

A right turn onto Main Street begins the ride into the city. Continue through town on streets until picking up a bicycle path at 25.2 miles. Paths then lead all the way back to Gallup Park. Ride over the one-lane wooden bridge into the parking lot, and you've sucessfully completed one half of A2.

The Cemetery Tour

Number of miles:	19.5
Approximate pedaling time:	3 hours
Terrain:	Rolling hills
Traffic:	Can be heavy on major roads during rush hour
Things to see:	Picturesque cemeteries, old barns, towns of Tecumseh, Macon, and Clinton
Food:	In Tecumseh, Macon, and Clinton

In southeast Michigan is a fantastic ride in the shape of an upside-down triangle featuring cemeteries at each corner—appropriate for a ride in late October. Actually, there is nothing spooky about it. The last two cemeteries on the ride offer paved small roads—paths really—that wind through the cemeteries; they're used by people in Clinton and Tecumseh for walking, jogging, and bicycling. They're treated as parks, and with all the trees, flowers, and ornamental headstones, they look like them, too.

If the thought of a cemetery tour is discomfiting, think of it as the "Great Big Barn Tour." Along curves and up and down hills, the ride passes some of the most picturesque barns in Michigan. And the ride takes you on good roads, with either a wide shoulder or a wide lane, and nearly all with light traffic.

Begin at Tecumseh High School and ride north. At 0.3 mile is the Douglas W. Bird Kiwanis Memorial Park, with benches, grills, paths, and a winding creek. There's water again at 2.8 miles, with a lake on the right. At 3.1 miles, the great barns begin, with one here and another 0.6 mile later, as the road curves left.

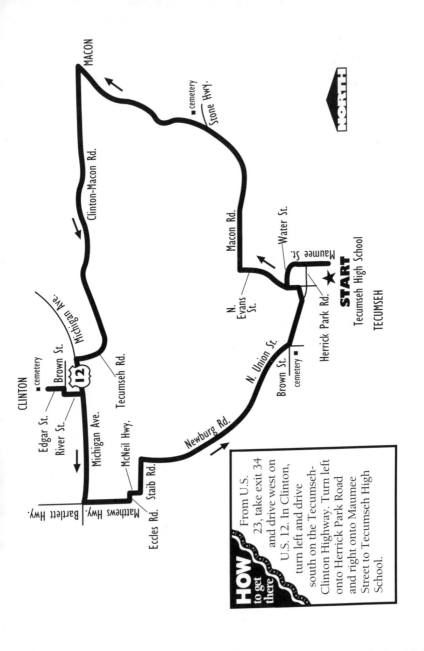

NORTH

MACON

Clinton-Macon Rd.

Stone Hwy.

■ cemetery

Macon Rd.

Water St.

N. Evans St.

Maumee St.

START

Tecumseh High School

Herrick Park Rd.

TECUMSEH

Michigan Ave.

CLINTON

■ cemetery

Brown St.

Edgar St.

River St.

12

Bartlett Hwy.

Michigan Ave.

Tecumseh Rd.

McNeil Hwy.

Matthews Hwy.

Eccles Rd.

Staib Rd.

Newburg Rd.

N. Union St.

Brown St.

■ cemetery

HOW to get there

From U.S. 23, take exit 34 and drive west on U.S. 12. In Clinton, turn left and drive south on the Tecumseh-Clinton Highway. Turn left onto Herrick Park Road and right onto Maumee Street to Tecumseh High School.

DIREC-TIONS at a glance

0.0	Turn left out of Tecumseh High School parking lot onto Maumee Street.
0.4	Road curves left and becomes Water Street.
0.5	Stop and turn right onto North Evans Street.
1.1	Turn right onto Macon Road.
3.9	Pull off onto Stone Highway to the right (to the left is Allen Road) for first cemetery.
6.4	At four-way stop, turn left onto Clinton-Macon Road.
11.3	Enter Clinton.
11.5	Stop and turn right onto Tecumseh Road.
11.9	Traffic light.
12.1	Cross Michigan Avenue (U.S. 12) at the traffic light and then turn left.
12.3	Turn right onto River Street.
12.4	Jog right onto Brown Street, then jog left onto Edgar Street.
12.5	Edgar Street dead-ends; cemetery entrance on left. When finished exploring, leave cemetery and backtrack to U.S. 12.
12.7	Stop and turn right onto U.S. 12.
13.2	Turn left onto Matthews Highway.
14.5	Turn left onto Eccles Road. Sharp curve right; Eccles Road becomes McNeil Highway.
15.7	Stop and turn left onto Staib Road.
16.1	Turn right onto Newburg Road.
17.8	Arrive in Tecumseh; road becomes North Union Street.
18.4	At four-way stop, veer right to remain on North Union Street.
18.5	Turn right into Brookside Cemetery. When leaving, turn left out of cemetery.
18.7	Stop and turn right onto Brown Street.
18.8	Cross railroad tracks.
19.1	Keep right at Y at traffic light, then go straight; road becomes Herrick Park Road.
19.2	Stop and turn right onto Maumee Street.
19.5	Return to Tecumseh High School parking lot.

At 3.9 miles, the first cemetery on the route is on the right. The smallest and perhaps the most charming, it rests atop a knoll. Trees line the right side, and a black wrought-iron fence surrounds it. The oldest stone is 1845, but perhaps the most poignant are three stones from 1860, when it appears that a mother died giving birth and her twins soon followed.

For those on the barn tour, look to your right at 5.4 miles. Trees line the road 0.4 mile later, as the gentle hills continue. Turn left onto Clinton-Macon Road. A mile later the road curves right and left with a wonderful barn here, also. At 8.1 miles, don't miss the barns with the green roofs. After a pond with a majestic weeping willow, at 8.5 miles, there's one of the longest hills on the ride. You're rewarded at the top with a cute red schoolhouse. Another hill, at 10.0 miles, is followed with curves and barns. The route enters Clinton 1.3 miles later.

After a right on Tecumseh Road, a shoulder begins. At 12.1 miles, cross Michigan Avenue (U.S. 12) and turn left to ride the sidewalk. This is the most traffic encountered on the route, so *use caution*. Take a quick right onto River Street, and the route visits the second cemetery. Pedal the wide paved paths as they meander among the headstones, or rest in the shade of a tall pine.

Ride back to Michigan Avenue and head west, crossing the Raisin River and passing a park on the left. A left turn onto Matthews Highway leaves the traffic behind. Turn left, at 14.5 miles, on Eccles Road—a dirt road in good shape. At the sharp right curve, it becomes McNeil Highway. Look left to see if the buffalo herd is visible. Mike Richardson, of the Adrian Maple Wheelers, says it's one of the ride's highlights. They are quite a sight. The pavement begins again on Staib Road.

The ride continues with hills, curves, and fabulous barns. Newburg Road, a right turn at 16.1 miles, leads to Tecumseh and the third and final cemetery. Brookside Cemetery, at 18.5 miles, is the largest cemetery on the route and has the most winding paths to explore. Head east through Tecumseh to Maumee Street, where a right turn leads past Bird Park and back to Tecumseh High School.

The Paint Creek Trail

Number of miles:	20.2
Approximate pedaling time:	3 hours
Terrain:	Flat on trail, rolling hills on roads
Traffic:	Avoid Orion Road and Adams Road at rush hour
Things to see:	Scenic views of Paint Creek, ponds, cedar swamps, Dinosaur Hill Nature Preserve, cider mill
Food:	Paint Creek Cider Mill, 3.9 miles; grocery store, 9.0 miles

The Paint Creek Trail beginnings go back to the 1800s, when a railroad was constructed on the route by the Detroit and Bay City Railroad. Over the years it was owned and operated by the Michigan Central Railroad, the New York Central, and finally the Penn Central, moving passengers and freight along Paint Creek.

The railroad ties have been removed, replaced with an easy-riding crushed stone, and footbridges, benches, and overlooks have been added, making the 8.5-mile trail one of the best rails-to-trails in the state.

Start by weaving northwest through Rochester Municipal Park, on one of the many paved paths to Ludlow Road. Cross the road and the creek to pick up Paint Creek Trail. The trail provides easy, flat riding, with plenty of curves to keep it interesting, as you don't know what wonderful view is coming up next. At 0.6 mile, pass the Dinosaur Hill Nature Preserve, with trails and picnic area. Then cross Tienken Road, at 1.0 mile, and the sound of traffic will be replaced with water babbling over the rocks of Paint Creek.

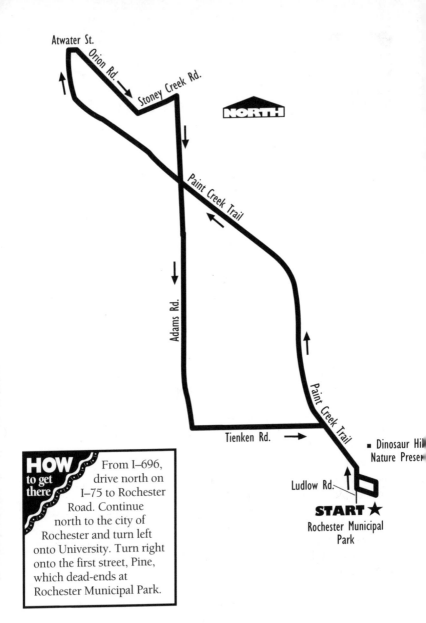

Atwater St.

Orion Rd.

Stoney Creek Rd.

NORTH

Paint Creek Trail

Adams Rd.

Paint Creek Trail

Tienken Rd.

Dinosaur Hill
Nature Preserve

Ludlow Rd.

START ★
Rochester Municipal
Park

HOW to get there
From I–696, drive north on I–75 to Rochester Road. Continue north to the city of Rochester and turn left onto University. Turn right onto the first street, Pine, which dead-ends at Rochester Municipal Park.

DIRECTIONS at a glance

0.0 Ride northwest through Rochester Municipal Park on paved paths to Ludlow Road.

0.4 Turn right onto Ludlow Road; walk bike on bridge over creek.

0.5 Turn left to cross street and begin riding on Paint Creek Trail.

0.6 Cross bridge and pass on right Dinosaur Hill Nature Preserve.

1.0 Cross Tienken Road.

1.2 Cross bridge.

2.0 Cross bridge.

2.2 Cross bridge.

2.3 Stop and continue straight on path after crossing street.Cross bridge.

2.6 Cross bridge.

2.9 Cross bridge.

3.2 Stop and continue straight on path after crossing street.

3.9 Paint Creek Cider Mill to right. Stop and continue straight on path after crossing street.

6.1 Stop and continue straight on path after crossing Adams Road.

7.0 Stop and cross driveway.

7.3 Cross bridge.

7.4 Cross bridge.

7.6 Stop and continue straight on path after crossing Clarkston Road.

8.5 Cross bridge. Path eventually narrows; continue straight.

9.0 Turn right onto Atwater Street.

9.5 Stop and turn right onto Orion Road.

10.0 Turn left onto Stoney Creek Road.

11.1 Turn right onto Adams Road.

12.6 Continue straight after four-way stop with Orion Road.

14.7 Continue straight after traffic light at Silver Bell Road.

15.7 Continue straight after traffic light at Dutton Road. Asphalt bike path begins.

16.8 Move into left-turn lane to turn left at traffic light at Tienken Road. If riding bike path, cross road and turn left.

17.3   Continue straight after traffic light at Brewster Road.

18.8   Continue straight after traffic light at Livernois Road.

19.2   At bottom of hill, turn right onto Paint Creek Trail.

19.6   Cross bridge at Dinosaur Hill Nature Preserve.

19.7   Stop and continue straight after crossing Ludlow Road.

19.9   Veer right at sign for Rochester Municipal Park. Turn left to ride paved path to parking lot.

20.2   Return to parking lot.

Wildflowers, grasses, and trees line the bridge-filled ride as the trail continues to cross and recross the creek. You'll pass plenty of fishermen scouting for trout in the creek as well as witness some of the work that they have done to preserve the area. The members of Clinton Valley Trout Unlimited have used timbers and rocks to shore up the banks of the creek, one of the few trout streams left in the area.

At 3.9 miles, turn right to visit one of the favorite stops on the ride: Paint Creek Cider Mill, which has cider, doughnuts, and other snacks as well as a complete restaurant. Continue straight to pass swamps and ponds, at 5.1 and 5.4 miles. Caution signs warn you to stay on the trail at 6.5 miles, as you move into an area used for archery. Beautiful tall grasses swaying in the wind alternate with ferns and trees.

The trail officially ends at 8.7 miles, as the path becomes narrow. But it's still fast going, riding straight, heading into Lake Orion. Ride under a canopy of trees before the path ends at a parking lot. Ride to the end and turn right onto Atwater Street. Riders may choose between the road and the cement sidewalk that leads to Orion Road, which is wide but has no paved shoulder. (If traffic is a concern, consider riding the trail back. It really does look different from another direction!)

Orion Road may be busy, but you're not on it very long, 0.5 mile, before a left turn onto Stoney Creek Road brings quieter surroundings. Ride a long uphill to a right turn onto Adams Road, which offers a wide shoulder. Begin with a long uphill, followed by a smaller down and up. At 12.2 miles, ride a long downhill on the way to the four-way stop with Orion Road. Continue the downhill as you pass the Paint Creek Trail at 12.7 miles.

Hills continue on Adams, as well as trees, fields, and horses, until a residential section at 15 miles into the tour. It's here a bike path begins—a good alternative if the road is busy. At 16.8 miles, a left turn on Tienken Road, which has a bike path as well, sends the route back toward Paint Creek. After several traffic lights and a few more hills, turn right onto the trail at 19.2 miles.

Follow the trail past a lovely view of the creek before ending the ride in Rochester Municipal Park. Here you can use the picnic tables on the tree-covered knolls. Drinking water and public rest rooms are available.

The Algonac Amble

Number of miles: 10.3
Approximate pedaling time: 1 hour
Terrain: Mostly flat
Traffic: Light
Things to see: St. Clair River and boardwalk, Riverfront Park, historic buildings
Food: Along St. Clair River Drive

Part of the St. Lawrence Seaway, the St. Clair River stars in this ride. The river connects Lake St. Clair and Lake Huron, and Algonac has built a superb boardwalk along its western bank. The ride includes the boardwalk and roads through woods and Algonac neighborhoods.

Turn left out of the Algonac High School parking lot, and head east on Taft Road. Ride either the wide sidewalk or the road through one of Algonac's residential areas. Turn left on Island Drive and make a quick right onto Fruit Road. Both of these roads offer a shoulder. The houses continue on Fruit Road, although there are more trees and tall grasses.

Turn left onto Nook Road, which dead-ends into Field Road, which has plenty of tall trees, curves, and small hills. At 3.4 miles, turn right onto Stone Road. The trees get thicker, and it feels like you are riding through a forest. A little more than a mile later is the turn onto Marsh Road, where the shoulder and trees continue.

Right turns onto Jankow and then Peters Roads, at 5.0 and 5.4 miles, lead the route through more trees and small hills. Both roads have shoulders and light traffic—a nice quiet stretch. A paved bike path begins after the left turn onto Mill Street, at 5.9 miles. More houses appear, but they sit back off the road, and there are enough trees to make it a quiet green section. At 6.3 miles, *use caution* at the

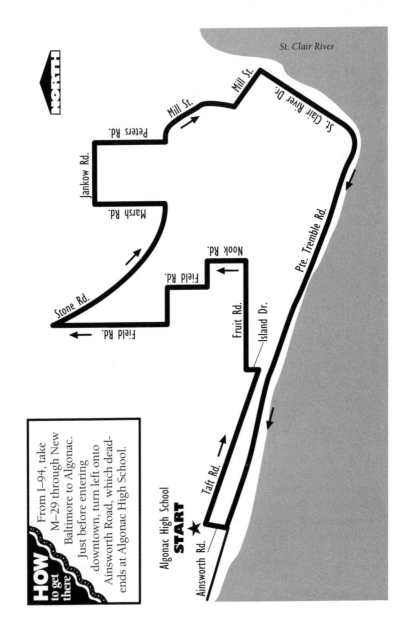

DIREC-TIONS at a glance

0.0	Turn left out of Algonac High School parking lot, heading east on Taft Road.
0.9	Stop and turn left onto Island Drive.
1.0	Turn right onto Fruit Road.
1.8	Stop and turn left onto Nook Road.
2.0	Stop and turn left onto Field Road.
3.4	Stop and turn right onto Stone Road.
4.5	Turn left onto Marsh Road.
5.0	Turn right onto Jankow Road.
5.4	Turn right onto Peters Road.
5.9	Turn left onto Mill Street.
6.3	Continue straight after three-way stop.
6.8	Turn right onto St. Clair River Drive.
10.2	Turn right onto Ainsworth Road.
10.3	Return to Algonac High School.

three-way stop—the northbound traffic doesn't stop. Curve right at the stop sign to stay on Mill Street. Soon the route approaches the St. Clair River.

At 6.8 miles, turn right onto St. Clair River Drive, M-29. Cross and ride the sidewalk, which will lead to the park. At Smith, River-front Park begins, and the route takes to the boardwalk along the St. Clair River. Across the street, wonderful old houses face the water.

Benches, flowers, and lights line the wide boardwalk. Plaques along the way tell the shipbuilding history of the area—sailboats, steamers, tugs, and cargo ships were built here, beginning in 1817. Approximately halfway down the boardwalk is the Clay Township Library, a beautiful building built around 1849 by Charles H. Beers.

The road curves right after the park and becomes Pte. Tremble Road. Continue on the sidewalk on the left side of the road. The grand old houses on the right give way to businesses. After crossing State, at 7.9 miles, a wide shoulder begins on both sides of the road. Cross here or wait until 10.2 miles, when a right turn onto Ainsworth Road brings the loop back to Algonac High School.

Ride Name	Great Lakes Ride	River Ride	Lighthouse Ride
1 Three Oaks Bicycle Museum Tour	●		
2 The Magical Mystery Tour			
3 It's a Grrrreat Ride!		●	
4 I Got a Ride in Kalamazoo		●	●
5 South Haven Side Ride		●	
6 Gunning Down at Yankee Springs			
7 The Saugatuck Sashay	●	●	
8 Tulip City Tour	●	●	●
9 The Coast Guard City Tour	●	●	●
10 Whitehall-Montague's Old Channel Trail	●	●	●
11 Lapping Lake Cadillac		●	
12 The Three Cs and a Circle			
13 The Glen Lake Gallop	●	●	
14 The Leland Loop			
15 The Old Mission Amble	●		●
16 The Lake Charlevoix Loop	●		
17 The Tunnel of Trees	●		
18 Circling Mackinac Island	●		
19 The De Tour Tour	●		
20 The Big Spring			
21 The Au Train Amble	●	●	
22 The Marquette Amble	●		●
23 A Superior Ride	●		
24 A Grand Ride at Presque Isle	●		●
25 Awesome Au Sable Amble		●	
26 Two Tawases and a Beach	●	●	
27 The Tip o' Thumb Tour	●		●
28 Inside the Thumb	●		
29 R&R in Bay City		●	
30 Riding the Pere Marquette		●	
31 Saginaw Sashay		●	
32 The Clio Creek Circuit		●	
33 The James S. Miner Riverwalk		●	
34 A Capital Ride on the Lansing River Trail		●	
35 Jackson's Portage Lake Loop			
36 The LakeLands Trail Loop			
37 To Hell and Back		●	
38 One Half of A2		●	
39 The Cemetery Tour		●	
40 The Paint Creek Trail		●	
41 The Algonac Amble		●	

*For a safe Family Ride, remain on bike path or trail and do not follow the route directions for off-path riding.

* Family Ride	Countryside Ride	Cityscape Ride	High Intensity Ride	
	•			1
	•			2
•		•		3
	•			4
•	•			5
	•			6
	•			7
•	•			8
	•			9
	•			10
	•			11
	•			12
	•			13
	•			14
	•			15
	•			16
	•			17
•	•			18
	•			19
	•			20
	•		•	21
	•		•	22
	•		•	23
	•			24
	•			25
•	•			26
	•			27
	•			28
•	•	•		29
•	•			30
•		•		31
•	•			32
•	•			33
•		•		34
	•			35
•	•			36
	•			37
	•	•		38
•	•	•		39
	•			40
	•			41

213

About the Author

An avid cyclist and a member of the League of Michigan Bicyclists, Pamela Stovall has pedaled roads and trails throughout Texas, Alaska, Florida, Costa Rica, and Ecuador. The beauty of her home state of Michigan, however, always brings her back, where she enjoys biking, hiking, skiing, and camping—almost anything outdoors.

Stovall, a writer and photographer, published her first book in 1992, *The Guide to American Vineyards*, followed by her second book in 1994, *Zero Proof: 200 Drinks from America's Best Bars and Restaurants*. Her articles have been seen in numerous magazines and newspapers, such as the *Dallas Times Herald, Accent Magazine, Woman's World, Association Trends, The Professional Communicator,* the *Austin (Texas) American–Statesman, Careers in Communications,* and the *Kodiak (Alaska) Daily Mirror.*

Stovall received her bachelor's degree, in political science, from the University of Michigan and her master's degree, in international communications, from the University of Texas. She has taught college classes in writing, English, and international communications.